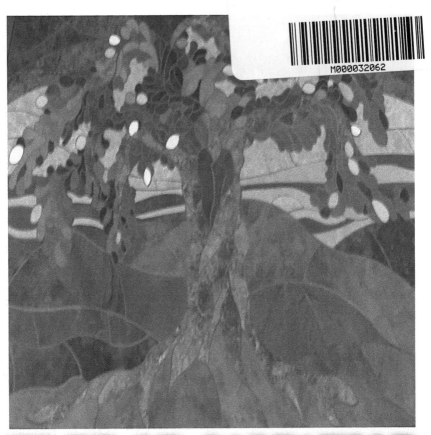

TREE OF SALVATION

My Journey Overcoming Addictions through Jesus Christ

Written by:

Dread Love

Illustrated by

Eliza Robinson, Mick Hassinger, Caleb Larkins, Nalini Pillai Casey,
Bethany Walker, Amy Lopez, Christian Probst, Dorthy Ledbetter

for us in the name of love. I count 9 points, but 7 equals Heavens. Have you ever seen the movie pie? It's a religious math movie. People make things way to complicated. Also I love tesla's theory of 3, 6, & 9 and how that is the key to understanding the mysteries of the universe. 3 judges, 6 takes & 9 recieves. lol simple math and everyone forgets about the 3 being grounded to the ground which equal the 12 tribes of Israel.

ISBN 978-1-64492-557-7 (paperback)
ISBN 978-1-64492-558-4 (digital)

Christian Faith Publishing, Inc.
832 Park Avenue
Meadville, PA 16335
www.christianfaithpublishing.com

Printed in the United States of America

I love the study of theology which are each really the study of basic math. Anyways if this book is a success then this is just a small part of what my next 2 books will write about

Illustration by Eliza Robinson

Anyways, thank you for being so awesome. I will forever love you. Love always,

931-206-7671

INTRODUCTION

"After being constantly drugged up, I lost my ability to eat, sleep, think clearly, and even talk. I remember hanging out with my brothers and friends, laughing, talking, and having fun. I remember in the back of my mind asking God, 'Why me?'"

"I'm not really sure how long I was out, but after standing up, I felt my eye swollen shut as well as my whole face hurting. Someone else said that I should lay back down saying I might have a broken neck. I lay back down and waited for the cops to come where I was later life-flighted to Vanderbilt Hospital."

"Nobody could trust me for what I had turned into and who I became. I remember one time asking my mom if I could stay there needing somewhere to sleep. She and her husband Mike (my stepdad) said, 'No way!'"

This is a story of my life, not only of my life, but also some of my favorite scriptures are in here as well as some quotes that I found very inspirational. There were many more scriptures and quotes that I wanted to add, but this is nearly an impossible task to do when there are so many to choose from. The scriptures are so wonderful; there are so many other great scriptures that I love as well. If any of the ones that I chose to use enlighten you at all, you can always open the scriptures and learn more about them for yourself. This is just a small piece of God's writing from some of His many prophets over the many years. I picked scriptures that stood out to me, as well as paralleled with my writing. Most of the quotes that I used came from a board that I would sit next to pretty regularly while I did some of my writing in rehab.

That is mostly what this story is about: my addiction recovery overcome through Jesus Christ! It tells just a handful of my many relapses over the years. It also shows how quickly I recovered once I decided for myself to fully walk into the light of Jesus Christ. How merciful He is to atone for my sins and to have the opportunity to feel His love daily. What an honor it is to know of His gospel, as well as a miracle to even still be alive, to feel, smell, taste, hear, and see life being on the better side of living for a change. It is never too late to turn your life around for the better, and I am a living example to share this story and let that be known. I had the most addictive personality in the world, so if I can do it, so can you! I can tell you too that being free of my addictions is the greatest feeling I have ever experienced, gaining the opportunity to feel my heavenly Father's love daily. With Him showing me why He brought me here, to grow into who He truly wanted me to be!

I have a dream to have my voice be heard. I have a dream that everybody treats each other as equals, as well as being there for each other, having a helping hand to love and comfort one another. I have a dream to make a difference in the world. What do you do when you have a dream? That's easy; you do everything you can do in your power to accomplish and make it happen! I felt as if God commanded me to write my life down and share my story. I felt this to be an impossible task and did not even know why I was asked to do this or what this story would even be about. "I can do all things through Christ who gives me strength" (Philippians 4:13). I started doing this task that I felt called to do, some years ago. Unfortunately, I lost that journal that I had started writing in but believe that part of my life was not really needed anyways. A lot of that writing was done while being heavily under the influence, therefore, it was cloudy thinking and not the best version of myself or my writing.

I, once again, started this task a second time while I was staying in a six-month inpatient rehab program. I, once again, had no idea what this story was to be about other than a journal of my life. I just felt as if I was supposed to write my life down.

Well, that is what I did and wrote more than I ever have in my whole life. After getting out of rehab, I was planning to finish my writing while working and living in Nashville. I thought it would be wise and in my best interest to move out of my hometown,

Clarksville, Tennessee. That still didn't prevent me from relapsing like I was hoping, and I did what I normally tend to do in my life. I gave up on my dream, this one being in writing, and went back to my old ways before ever having the chance to receive God's blessings. This is a snowball effect that has happened many times in my life; it starts out as one small mistake, and then rolls into a huge disaster. This seems to be an easier route to take sometimes, feeling like I didn't finish, therefore, didn't fail in what I put my entire heart into. This is something I have learned to be a trick and gets me nowhere in life having this kind of attitude.

When you have a task commanded by God to do, He does not allow this to continue happening. He made sure that I had gotten an excellent job after all the hard effort I had put towards sobriety and gave me the chance to have a great career. This job did not last long. I guess that was not the plan that God had in store for me. I ended up heavily relapsing, having another mental breakdown (this is something that has happened many times in my life, normally being stress related or drug-induced; most likely both), and once again, losing another journal. My sister and brother-in-law allowed me to stay with them, realizing the effort that I had put into the year prior to the incidents that I recently had. This was a great opportunity to have another fresh start and get my life in order to where it needed to be. I, once again, felt compelled to write my life down, and third time's a charm, right? This time in a more positive environment, with positive support, and feeling more diligent than I ever have in my whole entire life!

After nearly completing this task and finishing my life story, I had been trying to finish for years, I later found out that my brother, Sam, had received my other journal that I started in rehab. He works with the same company I used to work for, and that is where I last had it, leaving it in a company vehicle before nearly going to a psychiatric ward and ending up in a detox facility. At this point, my writing was nearly finished. I was also staying sober and going to church regularly. I had now gained a testimony of my church and of Jesus Christ. I had also figured out why I was supposed to write my life down and what the plot was supposed to be about: addiction recovery!

This story takes place in three stages of my life:

First is when I checked myself into rehab, now that I have my journal back in this writing.

Second is after I got out of rehab and stopped writing. (This will all come from memory and will be a mere few pages long in writing.)

Third is when I moved to Florida, got fully sober, and finished my writing while gaining a testimony of Jesus Christ in the process.

I have a dream of writing a story that somebody can read in one day that can drastically change their lives forever, maybe give them some hope or a better outlook on how they view themselves or their lives. The church that I go to, The Church of Jesus Christ of Latter Day Saints, teaches of our planet having ten thousand years of peace after the second coming of Jesus Christ. If you are not religious, maybe you can understand someone speaking for world peace.

Or you can enjoy some of the great quotes I have found from other great and inspirational people.

If you do not care about this either, maybe you can appreciate some of the beautiful artwork in here. Thanks to my artistic friends who share the same passion as me in wanting to make a difference in the world, I have this as well.

"Imagine all the people living for today. Imagine all the people living life in peace. Imagine all the people sharing all the world!" (John Lennon).

Journal While in Safe Harbor (Drug Rehab Facility)

January 24, 2016

"And now, as I said concerning faith—faith is not to have a perfect knowledge of things; therefore, if ye have faith ye hope for things which are not seen, which are true" (Alma 32–21).

F-eeling without Vision
A-ll
I-n
T-he
H-ands of the Lord

Illustration by Mick Hassinger

"Let your light so shine before men that they may see your good works and glorify your Father which is in heaven" (Matthew 5:16).

Illustration by Caleb Larkins

I am currently staying at Safe Harbor in Clarksville, Tennessee. It is a blessing that I am here. I have been an addict for the past ten years and have let drugs and alcohol run my life. Because of this, I have lost so much and have had continuous cycles of ups and downs. These are tricks from the devil. There is so much that I wanted to accomplish by the time I was twenty-five years old. I have had many falls by my drug relapses, preventing me from these dreams that I made for myself. Well I am not one to give up. To be realistic about it, there is no way that I can accomplish these goals, unless I overcome my biggest and really only problem that is getting in my way. This problem is: not putting my faith in GOD and breaking away from my addictions!

Illustration by Nalini Pillai Casey

BLUE

There once was a dog named Blue
Who liked to chew on my shoe
It made me real mad
The only pair that I had
See that pair of my shoe was new
What's one shoe of two
I grabbed that shoe, and I hit Blue
And then I got sad
For getting so mad
Blue didn't know
He was just a dog!

January 25, 2016

My friend from rehab named Tim wrote a song today and shared it with me after one of our church services. This is a faith-based rehab and part of the reason why I even agreed to check myself into a rehab, having the desire to also get closer to God. I felt so much heart in that song that I asked him if I could write it in my journal. I decided not to put this song in here but really enjoyed his lyrics. Music is something that really speaks to me. Especially when sometimes I feel so empty inside. I can't always tell if people are being my friend or my enemy. I know that I have relapsed quite a few times in my life, and it is a constant struggle for me every day! But I know when I search, ponder, and pray, Jesus Christ always tells me what is clear for me to do. His presence is such a glorious feeling. I can't even put into words how beautiful it feels. I know also that the devil hits me the hardest whenever I walk towards the light. I am so tired of falling and starting over. I would like to experience true happiness in Jesus Christ, if I am ever worthy enough for Him to allow this.

"Thank you God for being with me and in me—for feeling me with the HOLY SPIRIT!"

THE POWER OF ADDICTION
David Fritz (friend from rehab)

The day breaks dawn—given unto twilight,
The forbidden of night—reckoning of sight,
Love is a scripture that's ever untold,
We grow in the world to stay faithful and bold,
The power of addiction blatantly so,
The downward spiral on and on we go,
It controls our mind, makes as weak,
It makes us lie, steal, and cheat,
The oppositions of our sinful pride,
Masking our lives, we run to hide,
Running fast, betraying all that we love,
This bleeding past, I'm like a wingless dove,

Drugs have molded and shaped my sinful way,
Controlled like a puppet with strings of play.

January 27, 2016

God+Church+Family+Friends+Relationships+ Knowledge+Work+Love=life

Today was a successful day! I have gotten my job lined up to start soon through this program that I am in. I also went to court, and this went very well. I did some reading and writing, I got some exercise in, and had some good conversations with my fellow brothers here at Safe Harbor.

It is amazing how much impact that a positive outlook on life can be. Keeping Christ in my heart and staying away from false feelings or substances can really affect and help me for the better. It also helps to change my surroundings. I currently am not relapsing or withdrawing. My mood is not fluctuating up or down. It is only staying positive. The people inside this rehab are beginning to see the light that I am obtaining. I notice it as well! I am helping it to grow inside me by nourishing it daily. How do I nourish it? By searching the scriptures, pondering God's words, praying to Him, and keeping my faith in Him! HE WILL HELP ME in what I need help in. I am still struggling with nicotine, but this is not affecting me as badly as it has before in the past. I am confident that by the end of the week, nicotine will no longer be an addiction I have holding me down.

There was a paper given to us in one of our classes talking about employment skills. The way that it spoke to me was by the importance of what we do in each of our daily lives. How easy each day can be with family, friends, work, etc. if we stay positive and socially communicate in a happy, encouraging manner. On top of that, the preacher who led the discussion had a great message of Christ. He did this while emphasizing and having a lot of passion and soul in his teaching. This made it very spiritual to me, as well as very entertaining. I want to thank God for another successful day, as well as the change that He has brought me to in such a short period of time.

Everybody's got a past. The past does not equal the future unless you live there. (Tony Robbins)

It is not uncommon for people to spend their whole life waiting to start living! (Eckhart Tolle)

Owning our story and loving ourselves through that process is the bravest thing that we'll ever do. (Brene Brown)

Unused creativity is not benign, it metastasizes. It turns into grief, rage, judgments, sorrow, shame. (Brene Brown, PhD, LMSW)

When another person makes you suffer, it is because he suffers deeply within himself, and his suffering is spilling over. He does not need punishment; he needs help. (Thick Naht Hanh)

January 31, 2016

Today is Sunday, and I am currently in church. I have gotten a job working at Centurion Stone in Nashville, Tennessee. This is a factory job where we make stone-shaped concrete rocks that can be used for: stone walls, fireplaces, the outside of houses or buildings, etc. The list goes on. It can be used for pretty much anything that wants to have the appearance of stones as its texture. I used to think that I was a hard worker and had difficult jobs. After working this job, I think otherwise. I was wrong! It is very humbling to have a job like this. I have had many hard labor jobs in my life, but nothing compares to this job. This job is very fast-paced. To make it even worse, I am also working around lye. This leaves a chance of getting chemical burns on my skin if I am not careful. It has already happened to my friend, Derek Harris, who is in the program with me.

My position for this job is the start of an assembly line. Each assembly line has seven guys on a team.

It requires me to grab stone-shaped molds off a pallet (each mold weighs approximately 40 lbs.) and pass them onto a long row of rollers where they can each slide and be painted by two painters. After they are painted, they are flipped over so excess paint can fall off of them. They are then grabbed by the next two people in the line, who then fill the mold with wet concrete and hold them on a vibrating table. (This takes out any bubbles in the wet concrete that could mess up the rock's form.) Lastly, it is slid down another row of metal rollers, where another two people scrape off the excess concrete from the mold and carry it to another pallet. Each pallet is stacked eight molds high and four across, before taken off by a forklift to dry in a heated room.

On an eight-hour day of work, we have to do forty-seven of these pallets like this before we are finished. This is a lot of pallets to have to complete each day and is very fast-paced.

Illustration by Eliza Robinson

We are given only two breaks during the day: one fifteen-minute break and one thirty-minute break for lunch. Other than that, I am constantly moving the entire day. We are all moving in unison together, making me feel as if I am a robot. I make $30 a week to keep for myself; the rest of my check goes to Safe Harbor. It is agreed that I do this for the first ten weeks that I am in the program. After my ten weeks are up, I pay $130 a week for housing. I make $10 an hour. My goal is to walk out of this program a changed man, with a couple thousand dollars in my pocket to restart my life. I always have asked the Lord if I could have a job where I can get paid to exercise. He sure found me one! The Lord works in mysterious ways. This job that I am working, with the amount of money that I make, is very humbling. I know that there are also people in the world who are working even harder jobs. Some of them do this for even less money than I am making as well.

They do this without any kind of help and are even happy where they are at. I am very blessed to not have that kind of life. Some people live that way permanently for their entire lives, doing slave labor for little to no money. Americans take so much for granted!

I have quit all of my bad addictions except one which is nicotine. I am currently in church and am making my commitment to GOD to quit this one as well. By doing this gives me HOPE to receive more blessings from the Lord, by having FAITH that He will do so, if I commit to keeping His commandments.

> Wherefore, we search the prophets, and we
> have many revelations and the spirit of prophecy;
> and having all these witnesses we obtain a hope,
> and our faith become unshaken, insomuch that
> we truly can command in the name of Jesus and
> the very trees obey us, or the mountains, or the
> waves of the sea. (Jacob 4:6)

I have quit this addiction many of times in my life, but through my stupidity, I made the decision to relapse. (Thinking that this would be a onetime thing.)

I look at this addiction as a problem! If I do not have the will-power to quit such an unnecessary needing, with a constant chase, never-to-be-filled addiction, there is no way that I can walk back into the real world and be strong enough to not relapse and go back to my old ways. This is one addiction that makes me weak and vulnerable still! Well, I am currently in the Lord's house, it is time to stop writing and listen to His word.

Chew tobacco, chew tobacco, chew tobacco, QUIT!

H-elping

O-urselves

P-rogress

E-veryday

Illustrated by Bethany Walker

February 1, 2016

Today has felt like a pretty productive day. I went to work; my job is getting easier. I am starting to get the hang of this crazy work schedule and how each day goes. It is really not as hard as a job than I had thought it was when I first started. I just had to get back into the routine of working again. After work, I did a light workout, went to class, ate dinner, cleaned a bus that Safe Harbor just bought, did my daily chore that I am assigned weekly to do here (which is mopping the facility), then I did my laundry, and cleaned out my cubby where I store my items. The only downfall that I had was relapsing and smoking three cigarettes. This is something that I promised myself, and more importantly, promised God that I would not do. This is something easier said than done, I suppose. Hopefully, I can commit better tomorrow and not continue this silly habit of an addiction. It is useless, it costs money, and is slowly killing myself. This also goes against everything that I believe in. To stop smoking, all it requires is: TO HAVE THE WILLPOWER TO QUIT!

A good friend once told me that "every thought is a prayer; every action is an example!" His name is Adam Glenn. He is a very intelligent individual who has been through a lot in his life. He also served as a ranger for our U.S. Army. Another thing that he told me that I think about and has stuck with me is: "We are four-dimensional beings in a three-dimensional world." As I have pondered on this statement; it brings me to thinking about things I have learned through the church that I go to. This leads me to think about this same statement in a different way changing it to "We are Celestial beings in a telestial world."

I have tremendous respect for Adam. I met him at my brother's house whose name is also Adam. This was at his house in Nashville, Tennessee. I have tremendous respect for my brother Adam too. I have tremendous respect for all of my family members. They are all amazing people who have each been through so much. I will explain why later in this story but back to Adam Glenn. I am not entirely sure but believe that we ended up grappling that night. He is a mixed martial arts fighter and that is something I enjoy doing myself. I have a wrestling background from sixth to twelfth grade, and wrestling is a great background to have in MMA. This is also around the same time that this sport started growing and getting way more popular. We ended up hanging out a lot that night. The next day, he asked me about work. I currently did not have a job. He offered me a job, as well as a place to live. I found this too good to be true and assumed he was just talking himself up like people regularly do at parties. I later found out that he was being serious. After some time of living and working for him, he steered me towards finding a career for myself. This was just one blessing of many. Another way that I benefited from moving in with him was getting my own personal trainer who was a former boxer. There were other perks as well, but I will mention those ones later.

I am not one to write for long periods of time, but this could change later on as I continue this program. I will see if I even end up completing it and continue to do things that I feel I am supposed to do. I just wanted to mention one of my best friends who is a huge role model to me, who inspires me, and a huge inspiration to me in my life. If everything works out like I pray that it does, I will walk out of here a new and changed man. I will be somebody that I always knew that I could be, if I ever took the time to remember the Lord first and walk in the footsteps that He has already laid out for me.

B-asic

I-nstructions

B-efore

L-eaving

E-arth

Awakening is a shift in consciousness in which thinking and awareness separate. (Eckhart Tolle)

We are all broken, that's how the LIGHT gets in. (Ernest Hemingway)

No matter how many mistakes you make or how slow you progress, you're still ahead of everyone who isn't trying. (Tony Robbins)

I've learned that I still have a lot to learn. (Maya Angelou)

The thing that causes a deeper breakdown
than anything else is a denial of emotion. (Iyanla
Vanzant)

What we suffer now nothing compared to
the glory He will reveal to us later. (Romans 8:18)

Having courage does not mean we are...
UNAFRAID! (Maya Angelou)

February 8, 2016

Today is Monday, and I am at the courthouse waiting to see my probation officer. I am still struggling with nicotine. This is something that is really bothering me. I know that I can quit and will quit very soon. I know that once I accomplish this, I will receive further light and more blessings from the Lord. Every negative has a positive; every positive has more positives! I am not exactly sure where my life is headed, but I know that by keeping FAITH IN GOD, He will lead me exactly where I am needed. I live in a world where people tend to look past the higher power and even tend to deny the truth of our own existence. I am not much of a writer but am somebody with tremendous faith, have a positive outlook on life, and know that I have strongly personally felt the presence of our heavenly Father. There is NO DENYING the POWER of JESUS CHRIST!

Whenever I go to church and praise with my brothers and sisters through song, I get filled with the Holy Ghost; which is the spirit of Jesus Christ! It is the purest, cleanest, happiest feeling I have ever experienced in my entire life. Experiencing these feelings gives me enough courage and continues to give me HOPE to keep turning my life around. Sometimes, where I stay can be a very difficult environment to live in. There are people in this program who are not here by choice but are furloughed, being court ordered to be here. Some of the people who are not here by choice tend to be very negative and regularly talk bad about life and this program that we are in. Even with that being said, one thing that we do all still have in common is that we are all recovering addicts. This is something that is not a good thing but is good that we can all relate to each other in this way. The downside of this, however, is that through talking about our addictions, it ends up being the main focus of our conversations.

I know that I am guilty of this, and it is something that I am trying to change in myself. A lot of this is because I have done these things for so long, it is all that I know. It has pulled me away from my former passions that I used to have and remember caring about. Something that I enjoy about being here is the number of classes that we have on a daily basis. Public speakers will come and give knowledgeable talks and presentations on particular topics. Every topic that is discussed is always faith-based making it that much more powerful. One of the topics that was brought up last week that I really liked was how easy that it is to stay in our old ways. I am someone who likes change for the better and will pray that I will not continue to be the way that I have been living for years. It has been a struggle for me to quit some of my problems until I came into this program. Now that I am genuinely trying, it makes all the difference in the world. My entire thought process has changed, and I now feel more positive again. It is amazing what a little effort can do for someone that is trying.

Rapha's Twelve-Step Program for Overcoming Chemical Dependency:

Step 1:
   We admit that by ourselves we are powerless over chemical substances—that our lives have become unmanageable. "For I know that nothing good dwells in me, that is, in my flesh; for the wishing is present in me, but the doing of good is not" (Romans 7:18).
Step 2:
   We come to believe that GOD, through Jesus Christ, can restore us to sanity. "For it is God, who is at work in you, both to will and to work for his good pleasure" (Philippians 2:13).
Step 3:
   We make a decision to turn our lives over to GOD through Jesus Christ. "I urge you therefore, brethren by the

mercies of God, to present your bodies a living and holy sacrifice, acceptable to God, which is your spiritual service of worship" (Romans 12:1).

Step 4:

We make a searching and fearless moral inventory of ourselves. "Let us examine and prove our ways and let us return to the Lord" (Lamentations 3:40).

Step 5:

We admit to GOD, to ourselves, and to another human being the exact nature of our wrongs. "Therefore, confess your sins to one another, and pray for one another, so that you may be healed" (James 5:16).

Step 6:

We commit ourselves to obedience to GOD, desiring that He remove patterns of sin from our lives. "Humble yourselves in the presence of the Lord, and He will exalt you" (James 4:10).

Step 7:

We humbly ask GOD to renew our minds so that our sinful patterns can be transformed into patterns of righteousness. "And do not be conformed to this world, but be transformed by the renewing of your mind, that you may prove what the will of GOD is, that which is good and acceptable and perfect" (Romans 12:12).

Step 8:

We make a list of all persons we have harmed and became willing to make amends to them all. "And just as you want men to treat you, treat them in the same way" (Luke 6:31).

Step 9:

We make direct amends to such people where possible, except when doing so will injure them or others. "If therefore you are presenting your offering at the altar, and there remember that your brothers has something against you leave your offering there before the altar, and go your way, first be reconciled to your brother, and then come and present your offering" (Matthew 5:23–24).

Step 10:

    We continue to take personal inventory, and when we are wrong promptly admit it. "Therefore, let him who thinks he stands take heed lest he fall" (1 Corinthians 10:12).

Step 11:

    We seek to grow in our relationship with Jesus Christ through prayer, meditation, and obedience, praying for wisdom and power to carry out His will. "But if any of you lacks wisdom, let him ask of GOD, who gives to all men generously, and without reproach, and it will be given to him. But let him ask in faith without any doubting, for the one who doubts is like the surf of the sea driven and tossed by the wind" (James 1:5–6).

Step 12:

    Having had a spiritual awakening, we try to carry the message of Christ's grace and restoration power to others who are chemically dependent; and to practice these principles in all of our affairs. "Brethren, even if a man is caught in any trespass, you who are spiritual, restore such a one in a spirit of gentleness; Each one looking to yourself, lest you too be tempted" (Galatians 6:1).

February 13, 2016

Today I have officially completed one month of rehab at Safe Harbor. I am definitely happy that I decided to come here and am thankful for those that led me in this direction, suggesting that I should go to an inpatient rehab facility. This is, by far, one of the best decisions that I have made in a long time; if not in my entire life. It is really making a dramatic change in me for the better. Tim and Krista

Morgan are the ones that I have to thank for leading me here, as well as some of the closest support I have had around me this past year.

There is no telling where I would be at this point of time in my life if it was not for them. I am 100 percent sure that I would not even be here if it was not for their support.

There are plenty of others as well who helped guide me in wanting to change. I have been blessed in having great support in my surroundings of people who genuinely care about me. Enough to even pray for me by name, in hope to see me succeed. I feel the same way towards them, to the point that their happiness in life stays on my mind regularly. Even to the point that I continue to write the way that I do and keep a positive outlook in how I carry myself on a daily basis. I am, by no means, someone blessed with high intelligence, or in any way a superior writer. My spelling is bad, (thank you spell check computer!) I do not have the best vocabulary and, to be realistic, probably write as somebody from elementary school. A big part of why I believe to not be as smart as I could be is because of the decisions that I made for myself and what those decisions led me to do. I have made a lot of bad decisions leading me into bad situations. Life is all about DECISIONS!

The upside of this is that I am not one to stay thinking in a negative manner. It may sound crazy to say, but I am genuinely happy with everything that I have gone through in my life; through the good and the bad. If it was not for what I have gone through in my life, I would not be in any way, shape, or form who I am today. I am happy with who I am, what I have gone through, and having my dream of making a difference in the world. This plays a huge role in how I write as well. This is also a reason why I sometimes choose to copy down other people's writing of opinions and testimonies; knowing that each one has inspirational writing and a strong message in words that I could never express on my own.

If I did not write as if I was writing to somebody else, I would have no desire to continue my writing. I would probably give up on myself in writing, like I have done in so many other aspects throughout my life in this world. Writing is one of the many ways that I find peace and sanity for myself. It is very therapeutic for my heart, mind, and soul. There are also other tricks that I have up my sleeve as well, in doing these same things. There are many different ways that I help myself therapeutically. I enjoy helping other people to do this as well. This will sometimes give me confidence and boost my self-esteem in the process, knowing that I could help someone else benefit as well in life. (One of the tricks up my sleeve. I have many more!) All of this is done of course through communication! Communication is key for churches, families, friends, relationships, learning, work, and most importantly, towards our heavenly Father. If you communicate properly in all of these aspects of life, you will be guided and directed in what is necessary to be successful and even more importantly HAPPY IN LIFE! As a result, I gain positive feedback. This is definitely a miracle if you knew some of the people that I choose to surround myself with. Not that I have to explain because everyone knows of the world or fallen state that we are all living in.

Realistically, we are a highly advanced species of creatures that, in my opinion, could be much more advanced than the way we carry ourselves or even give ourselves credit for. We just have to tap into that part of our brain that over time has lost its ability to properly work. If we do this, it will help our bodies operate in ways we did not think possible. We just have to sync together our body, heart, mind, and spirit.

> And now, my brethren, I desire that ye shall plant this word in your hearts, and as it beginneth to swell even so nourish it by your faith. And behold, it will become a tree, springing up in you unto everlasting life. And then may God grant unto you that your burdens may be light, through the joy of his Son. And even all this can ye do if ye will. (Alma 33:23)

One thing that sticks with me and even kind of relates to this topic is something that my mom would say to me: "Love will overpower hate always!" I know this may sound random, but if you think about it, maybe not. This is a constant struggle or battle that people have every day. They may not be loving themselves enough or some-body else that deserves more credit.

Either one is a loss in my book and prevents you from progress-ing like you could be. I had the opportunity to see her today and am so thankful that I did. I love my mom so much and have her to thank for a lot of my positive outlook in life! Thanks for that message today, Mom!

Illustration by Mick Hassinger

It is getting late, so I am going to quit writing for the night, but tomorrow, I am going to write down a powerful message on communication from my close friend Justin (goes by JR), who is here in the program with me at Safe Harbor. He shared this with me and it is written by his brother. This is a very strong message and testimony that he has, so I believe it is worth being shared.

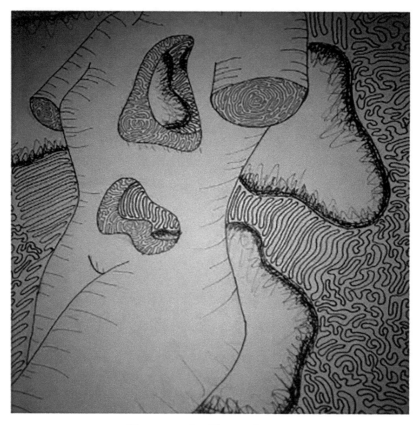

Illustration by Eliza Robinson

Ephesians Verse 29:

In verse 29, Paul says to **let no corrupt communication proceed from our mouths, unless it is good and is accompanied with the ministry of grace.** The age we live in today is full of communication. Bad or good, there are many avenues for communication. For the Christians, we are able to be vessels for good or corrupt communication. **(James 3 said out of the same mouth profess blessings**

and cursing. But if we are to be true to the holy calling in which we have been called to, then we must make it a practice to be aware of such discourse.) This verse raises several questions. What is corrupt communication? What is good communication? Can good communication also be corrupt? And how can I be effective in showing grace in my speech and approach? Is our duty as Christians to seek by God's blessings a way to communicate to others in order to get the unbelievers to think seriously about their ultimate destination and able to warn and comfort believers in a way that ushers them into God's loving mercy and grace.

What is corrupt communication?

By definition, corrupt here is translated as reproachful, injurious, useless, putrid, unsavory, hindering or obscene, unprofitable, all that is sinful, can also include profane oaths, curses, gossip, unchaste, hasty, proud, and naughty words, expressions that are mingled with conceit, a sense of pushiness, aggression or arrogance, lies, and perjury. Ephesians 5:4 also includes vulgar humor. These types of communication have the ability to leave a residue in the mind and the thoughts of the listener, causing present or future pollution in which can damage the heart and the spirit of man.

What is good communication?

Good communication is also known as something that is pure, profitable, pleasant. Words that instruct, counsel, comfort, promote repentance or increase faith, and establish hope.

Good communication is our ultimate goal. If we are able to maintain an unspotted form of communication, then we are able to speak the kingdom message that is accompanied with integrity and power. Let our conversation be wise and holy; filled with love that conveys grace or some divine influence. We must be pure of speech. God is pure. Our Savior is pure. The very lifestyle that we profess is a standard of purity set forth in scripture by God. We should never indulge ourselves in any obscene or negative act that would portray us as having a character that is contrary to who God has said we should be.

Can good communication be corrupt?

Absolutely! There will be times when we are engaged in a conversation or have an opportunity to minister that our good intentions can become corrupt and cause injury to the hearer. It is an easy thing to succumb to. There will be instances in which the hearer may not agree or may not be receptive to what we say, and if we become aggravated or get in a state where we are being really aggressive with trying to get our point across, we can easily open a door for evil to creep in and corrupt the whole situation. Even though we are speaking truth and we had good intentions, we must be sensitive to Holy Spirit's leading the words, motives, and emotions of all involved. (Colossians 4:6 says, "Let your speech be always with grace, seasoned with salt, that ye may know how ye ought to answer every man.")

There are several key things that can help us establish and maintain a biblical form of communication that is productive in displaying Godly character and effective in building the kingdom.

1. *Think before we speak.* We should never get caught up in being hasty to give a response. **(James 1:19 says to be quick to listen and slow to speak.)** There are times in which we should respond and times when we should hold our peace. We must be careful and not fall into Satan's snare, for he will speak lies in which will make us think that if we don't respond, then we are not ministering correctly. Or he may say things like you lack knowledge or sufficient counsel if you're not popping of scripture or have some response every time someone has approached you. There may even be times when you have a good response that is wrapped in truth but should still hold your peace. This is usually the case when you are dealing with those mentioned in **2 Timothy 2:23: "Foolish and unlearned questions avoid knowing that they gender strife."** In other words,

we need to not waste our time in debate. If given enough time, most conversations of this type generally tend to create unhealthy emotions or responses. There are, however, times when we are called to give good instruction. But it has its limitations also. For example, in **Titus 3:10–11, it says, "a man that is a heretic after the first and second reject admonition; knowing that he that is such is subverted, and sinneth, being condemned of himself." This is the person that after being given good Biblical counsel continues to ask silly and foolish questions in order to purposely stir up strife.)**

2. *We must ask ourselves, is what I'm about to say good?* Well that's an easy thing to gauge. We can measure that by our definition of corrupt. Is it reproachful, "condemning, or critical?" Is it destructive? Is it injurious? Is it negative? Will it hinder or promote welfare? Is it profane or foolish? Is it unholy? Is it encouraging? Is it obscene? Is it prideful? Is it hasty? Is it pushy? Is it truth? Is it vulgar? Is it gossip? The gossip thing can be very misleading, because I've heard many people say, "Well it's nothing I wouldn't say to their face." Really? That makes everything better? Even though you may be arrogant enough to speak the same words to that person directly, ask yourself this: When doing so, what kind of response might you get? Will they be overwhelmed with encouragement and jot, or might they be discouraged or hurt? We can easily identify the nature of our speech when we asked these questions.

3. Examine our heart. We must be able to see what fuels our conversations and what cause us to use the words we use. Our Lord gave a great example wit this expression in **Matthew 12:35–37: "A good man out of good treasure of the heart bringeth forth good fruit; an evil man out of evil treasure bringeth forth evil fruit."** But I say unto you that every idle word that men shall speak, they shall account thereof in the day of judgment. For by the words thou shalt be justified and by thy words thou shalt be con-

demned. We can likewise take this scripture and marry it with James 3 which says:

a) My brethren, be not many masters, knowing that we shall receive the greater condemnation.

b) For in many things we offend all. If any man offend not in word, the same is a perfect man, and able also to bridle the whole body.

c) Behold, we put bits in the horse's mouth, that they may obey us; and we turn about their whole body.

d) Behold also the ships, which though they be so great, and are driven of fierce winds, yet they are turned about with a very small helm, whithersoever the governor listeth.

e) Even so the tongue is a little member, and boasteth great things. Behold, how great a matter a little fire kindleth.

f) And the tongue is fire, a defileth the whole body, and setteth on fire the course of nature; And it is set fire of hell.

g) For every kind of beasts, and of birds, and of serpents, and of things of the sea, is tamed and hath been tamed of mankind.

h) But the tongue can no man tame; It is unruly evil, full of dead poison.

i) There with bless we God, even the Father; And therewith curse we men, which are made after the similitude of God.

j) Out of the same mouth proceedeth blessing and cursing. My brethren these things ought not so to be.

k) Both a fountain sends forth good at the same place sweet water and bitter?

l) Can the fig tree, my brethren, bear olive berries? Either a vine, figs? So can no fountain both yield salt water and fresh.

m) Truly indeed the tongue cannot be controlled by man but when man is controlled by the spirit and is in the submission to his prompting then the tongue can be a member of the body that can be fruitful and edifying.

4. When we speak, always use speech that is edifying and life giving. This can be done one simple way. Leave out your opinions, thoughts, and feelings and replace those things with the word of God. The wisdom of the word gives life. John 1 says:

   a) In the beginning was the word, and the word was with God, and the word was God.

   b) The same was in the beginning with God.

   c) All things were made by Him; and without Him was not anything made that was made.

   d) In Him was life; and the life was the light of men.

When God spoke forth the word and creation was established, life was formed when before there was a void. Our conversations should be within the parameters of the word of God. If we operate within these boundaries, our words are truly justified and good. Furthermore, we will have the power to create life in those who are seeking and searching for those voids in the mind and heart and soul to be FILLED! In the name of Jesus Christ, amen (testimony of Joseph Shockley).

Where there is anger, there is always pain, UNDERNEATH! (Eckhart Tolle)

Trade your expectation for appreciation and the WORLD CHANGES INSTANTLY! (Tony Robbins)

Do the best you can until you know better. Then when you know better, do better. (Author Unknown)

Imperfections are not inadequacies; they are reminders that we're all in this together. (Brene Brown)

Let faith be the bridge you build to overcome evil and welcome good! (Dr. Maya Angelou)

> When we strive to become BETTER than we
> are, everything around us becomes better, too.
> (Coelho, The Alchemist)

March 1, 2016

Today is the first day of March. This is an obvious statement by the date that I have written above. It has been some weeks that I have written other than some good quotes and a great testimony I received on communication. Writing is a hobby that I picked up, and I do not want to lose this good habit. I feel that it is necessary for me to write in order to keep the cycle of good habits flowing. It really bothers me to lose and stop doing a good habit that I have started for myself. This is something that I catch myself regularly repeating in doing over time. I will give up on good habits that I start, before I have the opportunity to see their blessings. Then, I will start this same cycle over again, and again leading me nowhere and keeping me where I am at. This is something I believe that many other people in this world do as well. A lot of times it seems easier to continue bad habits and keeping the same routine instead of changing things for the better. This is something keeping myself down and negative instead of up and positive.

Earlier, I took the time to read some of my writing since coming here. This is part of why I wanted to write, after looking at some of my progress since being here and having all of that information of what I have done fresh on my mind. I am not exactly sure how long I will be here, or what even comes next once I leave this program. I do have but a few goals for myself, as of now. First of all, I would like to have this journal full before I leave. Second and more importantly, I have been 100 percent sober since January 13th and want to keep it that way after I leave. This is huge progress coming from somebody that has been a severe addict for the past ten years of my life; nearly using some kind of substance every day. Third is to remain happy as this is the happiest I have been staying sober and can remember being in a long time. Fourth and last (the list keeps going on but I am too ADHD to write in steps like this), when I think of it, I will write whatever comes next to mind!

Since I have genuinely tried to turn my life around by receiving help and a support group (being with others wanting to do the same thing in their lives), life has truly become a lot sweeter. This is something that I have been told to be true, but how can I truly know something to be true until I personally experience it for myself?

Once starting this journey, I have learned this statement to be very true, and I am happy I get to see this side of life and experience it for the first time ever in my life.

March 14, 2016

There were some notes that I had taken about employment skills. I decided not to put them in the final editing of my writing. I will write things down like this when I believe it to be knowledgeable information that I want to obtain and keep for myself. I live in a world where work is a high percentage of our daily lives. It requires hard work inside and outside of our daily job to be successful in this world. It pays off to put in this kind of effort. As a result through daily diligence and time well spent, great results normally follow shortly after.

We live in a tough world! A place that can be judging at times and where people can act negative or "as haters!" Sometimes, in order to pull you away from that LIGHT, they may see inside of you. Misery loves company! We live in a world where people tend to care way too much about other people's opinions and how they feel about them. With people caring and feeling this way, it will often change how someone may act in a group; compared to one-on-one relationships. As a result, this can lead to mixed emotions in a relationship. This is why learning some of these psychology skills applied towards work (which was mentioned in the notes I decided not to use) and applying it in the real world can get somebody a long way in life.

Plus, the more you give yourself credit and positive feedback, the less that you care about your surroundings and how the rest of the world views you ask and thinks you may be. This is part of why I am very religious, knowing I have a protector always watching me. As long as I do what I know I am supposed to do and what is expected of me, I have NO FEAR and know that my Father in heaven is well-pleased. As long as I know He is happy with me, I am always happy with myself. If I am not happy, then I will ponder on why I am not, and God will always give me an answer of the reason why.

The more that you try for yourself and for others, the more confidence you will gain knowing you gave it your all. This confidence you gain is something that shines, and others begin to see it in you as well. I am led by the SPIRIT OF GOD in my writing and how I converse with others. This is something leaving me with no fear in what to say next, do, or how to act, because having God's Spirit with you is a powerful presence; the most powerful in the universe actually. Having this presence always on a daily basis is the most comforting feeling in the world. There are so many different blessings that the Lord has for each one of us. A couple examples on how God can bless you may be by giving you the ability to be telepathic or even see the future! These are just a couple examples; the list goes on and there are plenty more that come to mind! It will open up doors for you in ways you did not even think possible to gain in this life. Windows of opportunity will immediately become crystal-clear in your thinking. Do flowers not bloom overnight?

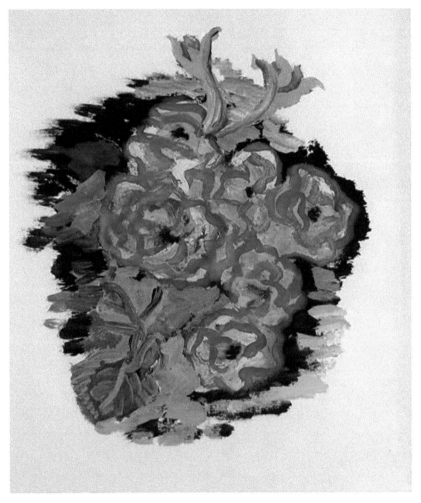

Illustration by Amy Lopez

This is why confidence in this world will get you a long way. This is also why diligence is an important skill to obtain for yourself. The more that you try, the more you will learn you can do, and things will open up to you that you never imagined possible. You will start to realize the doubts you once had are no longer there. You will begin to forget about your worries and problems. You will also help others in the process of helping yourself without even realizing it, or the blessings that you are beginning to receive. Love beats hate every time (thanks again for that knowledge mammal). I forever love you! To go along with doing what you are supposed to, you will begin to climb a mountain of opportunities and see things you have never seen before! You will obtain ENERGY like you never imagined possible! It may start out a little difficult for some to change; it may be a struggle. The start of this mountain may be slow with a steep start to climb, but the harder that you try, the more effort and work you put into it, the easier it becomes. And I promise you this: blessings will come like you never imagined possible and OTHERS WILL FOLLOW YOUR FOOTSTEPS!

> If you can't fly, then run. If you can't run, then walk. If you can't walk, then crawl. But whatever you do, keep moving forward. (Martin Luther King Jr.)
>
> One thorn of experience is worth a whole wilderness of warning. (James Russell Lowell)

March 26, 2016

Today was a good day! I got to take a Saturday off from work. I've been working Saturdays through my job to receive more money. My goal is to leave this program with a few thousand dollars in my pocket and to be physically, mentally, and spiritually stronger! I want to become a changed man. I'm ready to travel the country with my brother, having a new mentality in life, and ready to see the world with a whole new aspect. Writing like I do is a big help for that.

I was hoping to leave in April. That's when I have my next court date. I believe if I told the judge my plans, he would most likely allow it to happen and release me from probation. That is a major reason why I am still living in Clarksville like I am, but what brought me into this program was a call for help in wanting sobriety. That goal is what I find most important for my life right now, as well as gaining a closer relationship with God. Both of these goals started to happen the day that I came into this program. I am receiving more blessings than I believed possible in such a short period of time. God is good!

I've always had strong beliefs in His power but never received His grace in full because of my daily actions. I am now beginning to see how His power can truly work if you truly let Him work in you!

I plan to not mention anything to the judge about wanting unsupervised probation and leaving the state. If I wait till July, then I will have graduated the program that I am in, as well as getting off probation that same month. That will leave me with a completion in both of those areas and leave me with nothing else to have to look back on.

I tend to quit a lot of things that I try to start for myself, not seeing the final steps of where that outcome could have led me. This is the happiest I have seen myself in a long time (maybe ever). I would like to see the final results of where it may lead me! There is a strong brotherhood here. Some of the strongest I have ever seen with so many different types of personalities and types of people, all connected through our similar backgrounds and what we've been through with many of the same addictions. All putting faith in Jesus Christ as well as each other to help get past our struggles and grow from what we've been through! That is a powerful experience to have as well as some of the best support you can imagine! I would feel like not completing this program would let some of my brothers here down as well as myself. I look up to them as they do me. "God gives His greatest battles to His greatest warriors" (a quote one of my brothers said in class).

Today a good number of us all left the mission and went up the road to go bowling. That was part of why I missed work today. It's good to take breaks from your daily schedule/routine sometimes and give your body and mind a chance to rest and recover from what you may feel sometimes obligated or expected to do. Sometimes, I feel like people get too caught up in what they feel is necessary for themselves, friends, family, or loved ones and prevents them from enjoying things that they love doing most in life. Sometimes, the outcome of these actions can put someone in a bad mood, leaving them a negative attitude about life, and teaching them to fight with who they care about most in their life, or can even lead to gaining unhealthy addictions for themselves. (Not only substance abuse.) It can be as simple as overcleaning something! Turning it into an obsessive problem rather than a healthy process. There can also be positive addictions. Just ask yourself: Is this helping me? Do I enjoy doing this? Is it taking away from things more important? Is it negatively affecting people in my life that I care about the most? Is it turning into a problem rather than an inspiration?

You can be your best friend or your worst enemy! You control the fate of your future and your life! Sometimes, I like exclamation marks if you can't tell. It makes me feel like I'm getting my point across in a stronger manner.

Tomorrow, I celebrate the resurrection of my Savior. His death was out of love for us to allow us to repent, be forgiven, and worthy to have eternal salvation in His light and glory. As He resurrected, we too will have that same opportunity, walking in His path of eternal paradise with Him. So beautiful! True love!

I'm looking forward to celebrating and remembering what He's done by His grace and plan of salvation for us. Anyone who denies His existence on what has already happened and what He's done is an ignorant fool. They are missing out on what He offers, His plan for them, and how much of a difference there can be in His light. I missed out for years on things I could have received and had happen in my life. I also understand as well that it happened differently though, because I could handle what I've been through (knowing I could handle it) to strengthen me and make me who I am today as well as who I am becoming.

Tomorrow, I also get to have a five-hour pass to go out and get a chance to see some of the people that I care about most in this world. I'll be with my mom, stepdad, two of my brothers, and my sister and her kids. It's been a long time since I've gotten to see that many family members at one time. (Other than my parents, my siblings have moved to different parts of the country, all being a good distance away). This will also be the first time since I was a kid that I'll be this clear-minded and sober to spend time with any of my family. I'm excited to see if they see any difference in me like I see in myself. Over the years, I have made a lot of mistakes continuously in my life, leaving them to lose my trust as well as constantly worrying about me. I hope they see that I'm trying to change for the better. I love them so much and am sorry for the stress I've caused them over the years. This is a big part of why I am here. Sometimes it's easier to change your ways for others than for yourself.

> Life is like riding a bicycle. In order to keep your balance, you MUST keep moving. (Anonymous)
> When you get, give. When you learn, teach. (Maya Angelou)
> All great changes are preceded by chaos! (Author Unknown)
> When we deny the story, it defines us. (Anonymous)
> When we own the story, we can write a brave new ending. (Brene Brown)
> Rock bottom became the solid foundation on which I rebuilt my life. (J.K. Rowling)
> Loving ourselves through the process of owning our story is the bravest thing we'll ever do. (Brene Brown)
> The tragedy of life is not death but what we let die inside of us while we live. (Anonymous)

April7, 2016

Today is Thursday, and it is just after 12:00 pm. I have court at 1:30. It is the first time in my life that I am going to appear in court and not have mixed emotions on how the outcome of it is going to turn out. I am pretty confident that it will go well in my favor. Last time that I went, the judge told me that this is my one chance to get my life in order. He said this after I told him that I'm in a rehab at Safe Harbor. I told him that I needed help and that I have problems. I also told him that I am getting the help necessary to break the chains that are holding me back and keeping me down. I have been at Safe Harbor since that last conversation with the judge, who decides the outcome of my freedom. With me continuing this program, I am confident that the final results of my freedom will be finalized in good terms.

Positive Thinking = Positive Energy & Positive Results

Illustration by Christian Probst

There have been some good things that have happened these past few weeks that I haven't yet had the chance to write down. Sometimes, I procrastinate and put important things off instead of focusing on them. I was able to see two of my brothers and my sister and her kids at Easter. We all went to church together with my mom and stepdad. One of my brothers, Adam, it was his first time going to church in years. It was really cool to be there with him when he came as well as another brother, Johnny, Mary Kay, her two sons (my nephews), Carter and Hyrum, and my niece, Emmary, (Emmy). That was my first time meeting Emmy, and I got to hold her for a little while when my sister and her oldest son, Carter, did a duet together for the church. She played the piano and he sang "I Am a Child of God" first in English, then again in Spanish. Such a smart kid at only five years old! My sister is a great mom, giving her kids lots of knowledge and showing them the importance of religion and attending church. (I have found this to be a huge blessing in your life if you follow God's commandments.) Adam also brought with him his fiancé and her me-maw (grandmother, how we say it in the south!) I thought that was special as well. Before my rehab pass was over, my brother wanted to see our father before he took me back there. We had been fighting the last time I talked to him months earlier, and I hadn't really spoke with him since then.

It was good that we talked again, and he knows that I am in rehab getting the help that I need to give myself a better life. We left each other on good terms and that made me happy to know that everyone in my family is proud to see that I am trying to make better changes in my life on the sober path, keeping the Lord in my heart.

It turned out to be a great Easter. To top it all off, I had a very spiritual moment with Christ that I want to explain in detail. (Sorry this story was out of order but like I've said, I am extremely ADHD and tend to write down what comes to mind first.) On Easter Sunday, the greatest thing that happened was during the church song we sung before we partook of the sacrament (representing the body and blood of Christ). I just remember singing the song of Christ in Gethsemane and His eternal sacrifice. Right before the last verse of the song, I broke into tears and had to stop singing! I cried most of the way through the following prayer. It was one of the cleanest, most peaceful feelings that I have felt, longer than I can ever remember. It gave me hope! It gave me faith in The Church of Jesus Christ of Latter Day Saints, which is the church that I grew up in. This was the church I was raised into and feeling that much peace while being there, told me that this church does have modern truths of the Christian faith. With that much peace in that moment, it told me this is the true church of God. It really strengthened my testimony and gave me the desire to continue learning and walking in the path of Jesus Christ. I know that the Lord is and always will be 100 percent real. He is ALWAYS here, He is always there, He is everywhere, waiting for me (or you!) to call on Him.

That was the highlight of my Easter Sunday! Having tears of joy with Jesus Christ, feeling His glory and presence, knowing that He is in my life right there when I need Him, waiting to see if I will do the right thing and walk towards HIS LIGHT! He will never give up on me no matter what I do. He died on the cross for me, when I am not worthy. Because of that, I will eternally pray to Him, treat others with kindness, and sing to Him with JOY! These were some important things that had happened to me recently in my life that I felt the need necessary to write down and something I have put off doing.

Court also went well! The judge continued my court date to July 14. That is the day after I complete this program. He wants to see me finish it through, as well as complete the rest of my probation that I have left. I will be done with probation on July 5, I will be done with Safe Harbor July 13, and be a free man hoping to put my problems in the past on July 14. I am grateful to be where I am at. I am blessed to be in the program that I am in. Thanks to the people that led me here, as well as the people that are in here with me, I am learning a lot and growing in so many aspects of my life. I am putting my faith in Jesus Christ knowing that there are blessings in store for me and that He does perform miracles. I have seen them happen! The people in here with me (other former addicts) are a huge inspiration to me and being here with them is a very powerful force to be a part of experiencing. Each and every one of them having a strong testimony of Jesus Christ! There are former addicts who volunteer their time to come here and share their story. They do this in hope that each one of us will grow from it and succeed in being here, as well as leaving here. They come and share different stories on how they gained a testimony of Jesus Christ and how He worked miracles in each of their lives. They would come in and ask if there was anybody here wanting a prayer by name, so that they could pray with us for each one of them.

I am so thankful to be here. I have seen so many different changes in myself, as well as in others that are here with me. I have grown so much mentally, physically, and most importantly, spiritually. There have been so many positive changes I have seen in just a few months; it is truly a miracle. I know I still have a long way to go but also know and have faith that it is speedily coming. The Lord is truly answering my prayers in a very short period of time. I am beginning to see some things that I have asked for, become answered.

It is amazing what the Lord can do for you if you knock at His door and allow Him to be a part of your life. HE IS REAL! He is just as real as you are, or me! This writing is a huge part of my rehab. What is an addiction? Something affecting you negatively on a daily basis! If my story can make a difference in someone else's life as well as bring them to life in the light of Jesus Christ, then it is a small price to pay to conquer my addictions and share my story to anyone that may listen and benefit from what I say.

I am eternally grateful if I help even one person through their trials. Life is too short to waste away in sorrow wishing things could be different before it is too late. Life is a beautiful creation to be a part of living. It can be even better too, if we all worked together as a team and allowed it to work in ways that I know are possible. Why does everybody only care about themselves or direct family? Aren't we all part of the same family tree? We have our ups and our downs, but these are learning experiences for us to grow. We are also eternally blessed through going through these trials and errors. We either choose to learn or continue to be punished. We have the free agency to choose the path we desire: good or evil, right or wrong, love or hate! These are powerful emotions we have to choose from and tremendous knowledge to gain through each experience that we go through! I am by no means a typical saint! I make a lot of bad choices and decisions! I am at the point in my life of weighing out my pros and my cons in what I should do next! I have come to a conclusion of trying out the path of Jesus Christ. There is nothing negative to come from this decision. I have tried out many bad decisions in my life. Why not try out a good decision for a change? I may mess up and have some trials, but the difference is that I will never keep myself down like I have in my past and give up!

Illustration by Amy Lopez

The danger of grappling with the beast is that you might become one. (Anonymous)

Luck is when opportunity meets preparation. (Anonymous)

But this one thing I do, forgetting those things which are behind, and reaching forth unto those things which are before. (Philippians 3:13)

July 4, 2016

Today is the fourth of July, and I have about a week and a half left in this rehabilitation program that I am currently in. After that becomes my test of coming back into the real world. I will be back on my own again, and the next test begins with what decisions that I choose to make having full freedom again. This is what life's about: having the choice to make decisions and learning through the outcome of where these decisions lead me. My head is not really in the mindset to be writing, but I read some good quotes that I wanted to write down, and the Spirit led me to do so. I am also very close to being done in this program.

This is an important part of my recovery, writing like I do. I feel the need to write down the last bit of my time here and how it has been going for me. It gives me a bit of self-satisfaction in doing this. My friend, Justin, who goes by JR ended up leaving the program early. He was supposed to help me with some illustrations in this story. That ended up not happening. I am a very visual individual and think that beautiful artwork would add so much to my artistic words. Hoping that it may help more to visualize what I am writing down. I had a dream to write an adult picture book with creative pictures to go page to page with my writing. Just as a children's book would be, only way more artistic and advanced. I know also that I sometimes tend to get bored with books and having a book full of pictures may be enough to keep my eye on what I open up.

Anyways, that did not work out, so I guess now is not the time or place for that to happen yet. Everything that I had planned once leaving here fell through. I was not able to get a job with my brothers doing cell phone tower work. My plan is to continue the job that I currently have, move to Nashville (getting me away from Clarksville my hometown), and have my own place. This will be the start of my new life having a fresh start, coming out of six months of recovery. Coming to this rehab has done me a lot of good. It gave me a lot of time to focus on myself and what I want to have in my life once leaving here. Right now, there is not a whole lot that I expect to have for myself coming fresh out of a recovery program like I am in, but here are a few things that I plan on having for myself once leaving here:

I want to have my own place, so, in order to have that, I am going to settle with living in a hotel, so I can immediately have that once I leave. Not having any furniture or a car this seems like the best idea, being close to my work, and having everything I need for a bedroom.

1. I want to continue my weekly exercises in keeping my body toned, in shape, and growing in the way that I am wanting it to grow. Also, I exercise for the endorphins and dopamine that it releases; giving me the personality I like, staying positive, as well as sane (this is half the reason of why I like to work out).

2. I want to be in a new city and be able to save up money. Wanting these two things is enough to settle for the slave job that I have in order to make both of those things happen. Hard work is rewarding!

3. Last but not least, I would like to finish filling out this journal with my story of recovery being a success and maintaining a happy, successful life for myself. Well, this is all that I have to write for today out of my personal life. I still might have a couple of more things to write this evening, but they will not be my words.

4. Just like the start of my journal I find things that I enjoy reading and write them down. This is mindless work that helps me maintain and keep information that I find is important in life.

My past does not control my future. My past is only a place of reference, NOT a place of residence. (Author Unknown)

Promise Yourself
Author Unknown

Promise yourself to be so strong that nothing
can disturb your peace of mind.
To talk health, happiness, and prosperity to every person you meet
To make all your friends feel that there is something in them.
To look at the sunny side of everything and
make your optimism come true.
To think only the best, to work only for the
best, and to expect only the best.
To be just as enthusiastic about the success of
others as you are about your own.
To forget the mistakes of the past and press
on to the greater achievements of the
future.
To wear a cheerful countenance at all times and
give every living creature you meet a
smile! :)
To give so much time to the improvement of
yourself that you have no time to criticize
others!
To be too large for worry, too noble for anger,
too strong for fear, and too happy to
permit the presence of trouble.

2

After Leaving Rehab

August–November 2016

This all comes from memory, but I am currently sober and have a clear memory of everything worth putting down in my journey after rehab. As I was finishing rehab, I had one last court date before the judge. I came before him when my name was called. I had already finished probation and also had the last of my probation fees paid this morning. This was the least worried I have ever been going to court. I knew that I had been doing everything in my power to becoming a better person and also doing what was expected of me from the court. As I appeared before the judge, I had someone through the court represent me and tell the judge my progress. Judge Grimes told me that he was shocked that I finished probation and even more shocked that I stayed in rehab for six months. He told me that he was very well pleased with me and was going to personally tell Judge Shelton my progress. (These were the two judges that I had seen the most over the years.)

Hearing these words from the judge and knowing that I had gained my freedom back in every aspect possible was an amazing feeling. I felt a huge burden taken off my shoulders and felt like a free man once again. It had been years that I did not have to worry about being in trouble with the court or looking over my shoulders. I remember that being an amazing day. After taking care of court,

I now could move forward in my life, having nothing to look back on. I also was free from rehab and could do whatever I wanted after getting out of court. I wish that I could say that I was staying 100 percent sober but in this case, that would not be true. Even though I was not hooked on heavy drugs like I had been in the past, I was still addicted to alcohol and nicotine. I was also still using some drugs on occasion as well.

As bad as it sounds, still having these addictions after leaving rehab was actually huge progress compared to how much worse I was before going into this program. I was using multiple heavy drugs weekly and drinking daily sunup to sundown. Now, I was only drinking weekly not daily. I know it does not sound much better, but it really was an improvement. I also had a job in Nashville and had the plan to move there getting me away from easier access to drugs. I later found out that this would still not keep me away from these bad habits. Some of these addictions that I had were still talked about during work, and there were a lot of addicts who both sold and used where I worked at. I was once again regularly using certain things that I should be staying away from. I did, however, gain enough willpower to not become completely broke or go overboard in these addictions again. I discovered while in rehab how much I enjoyed eating good food, so promised myself that even if I do mess up, I would never go broke and blow my paycheck that same day.

I did at least stay committed to that promise that I gave myself. Even if I did occasionally buy something that I shouldn't be buying or drank pretty regularly, I always made sure I had a decent amount of money to eat during the week. This is coming from somebody who would blow my whole paycheck the day that I got paid. I was even paying $275 a week in rent (which was what I was used to paying monthly) and was still having more money than I was used to having. I was also working between fifty-eight to seventy-five hours a week. This gave me a pretty fat paycheck and kept me plenty busy which also helped keep me out of trouble. This was a very hard job, and I once again felt trapped, wondering what I was going to do next with my future. What was I going to do the rest of my life? I had knowledge in massage therapy and electricity, but I was settling for a mindless, hard laboring, factory job! I knew that I could be doing so much more with my life. I am not a settler; I knew this would work for now, but what comes next?

Even with me messing up like I just talked about, I was still doing better than before. I would meet with the sister missionaries on occasion and also, sometimes go to church on Sundays. I had not forgotten about God and was trying my hardest to keep Him in my heart. I knew that I was still messing up but also realized how much that I progressed this year in a short amount of time. I had Him to thank for my progress and for bringing me back to being a happy and more hopeful person, like I remember being in my past. I knew that I wasn't doing as well as I could be, but I have also seen myself a lot worse.

I made sure that I regularly prayed and tried to read the scriptures when I could. I always kept the Lord in my heart and because of that I believe I was blessed to be a positive thinker. I can feel trapped and have literally next to nothing going on in my life but appear to be the happiest person in the world. This is because money doesn't buy happiness; happiness comes from within, and only you have the power to keep yourself happy. If you put your faith in God, He will give you what you want! Do I want to be successful? Are there certain goals and accomplishments that I want in life? Well, of course! Why wouldn't I want these things? The two most important things that I want in my life are already there and always will be and takes little to no effort to maintain. The two things that I find most important to have in life is to stay happy, keeping a positive outlook in life and to have a relationship with my Father in heaven. As long as I continue to keep a relationship with the Lord, He blesses me with happiness (even if there is nothing else going on in my life).

He has also inspired me to write my life down. After having a few intellectual people read my testimony at the end, they have inspired me to feel as if I have intelligent writing. That I actually may have written something that could help people in their lives. My brother-in-law, Tim, was a great support on this. He listens to Grant Cardone and other inspirational writers and speakers all the time. Tim is a self-made business owner at the age of thirty-three. He is the husband to my sister, and together, they are one of the strongest couples that I have ever met. They are very strong in all three aspects that I continue to write about: physically, mentally, spiritually. If they did not give me the confidence in saying that I could do this, I would have already forgotten about it and gave up on this dream. They truly saved my life! I am forever grateful. One thing Tim told me that really made me feel good about what I am doing and to not give up on myself was this: "Even if your story does not go anywhere, it was still a great accomplishment!" These were words that I needed to hear after being self-conscious in my efforts of trying to publish a book.

Anyways, back to me being in Nashville. Like I said before, I was not staying sober but was doing better than I have been in my past. After keeping this job so long, I became blessed, and my brother came through in getting me a job in cell phone towers just like he had promised. Thanks, Adam. You came through for me brother. I love you! (He got married to his wife, Melanie, shortly after I came out of rehab. I was really drunk at the wedding and that made a lot of my family sad seeing me that far off after just leaving rehab.) I was not able to work on the same crew that he was on but had gotten a job through the same company, Encode. I was soon picked up in Nashville, quit my job at Centurion Stone, and was shipped to Georgia to be trained. Before I could start working for them, I had to get some training in and receive some certifications required to have to be on site. I was a little nervous about these tests that I had to take (not being the greatest test taker), but still believed in myself, and knew that when there's a will, there's a way! And to my surprise, I passed all my tests with flying colors.

I impressed everyone in the company in how fast I completed my tests, as well as myself. Soon, we were ready to begin some of these sites. As time went on, I impressed the company with how quickly I learned how to use the equipment in testing our installations. I also learned all the requirements necessary to pass and complete each site that we did.

I was training people who had years of experience beyond me. They had experience in climbing the towers. They were used to installations on the tower in the air. We were doing ground work and installing new equipment in the shelter next to the cell phone tower. These were two completely different styles of work. I paid better attention in our training of how to install the equipment, therefore, even with their experience, I still had the greater knowledge.

Life was looking well for me. I was better off financially than I had been in my entire life, having the best career of my life. I was riding around in a brand-new 2016 Dodge truck. I was getting per diem on top of my hourly pay, as well as extra cents added to my hourly pay for the number of miles we had to drive weekly. I was staying in pretty nice hotels paid for by the company, I was getting lots of hours, I was working inside an air-conditioned room where I did a lot of the work sitting down, and I was making the most amount of money in my life working the least amount physically. I was always on the road barely spending money because I never needed to because I was always working. I felt truly blessed! God is good! He blessed me for trying as hard as I did this year.

After working this job and learning it very well, I soon had the opportunity to come home on weekends. My friend that I was working with asked to come home on weekends so that he could spend some time with his family. (It was also so he could stock up on certain supplements to have throughout the work week.) One of the things that he enjoyed doing was something that I also liked to do. He asked me if I could find it for him. I stupidly agreed that I would, wanting to dabble a little in this substance as well. I told myself that it would be a onetime thing and that I would not let it lead to a problem again. That clearly was not something that I was capable of doing. Before I knew it, I was once again doing the main thing that led me to rehab.

I would stay up all night Friday driving from Georgia to Tennessee, get to my hometown Saturday morning, get what I was planning on getting once, and stay up the rest of the weekend, even until I came back to work Monday. I would sometimes work the job that I had from as early as six o'clock in the morning until sometimes eleven at night. This would be how long my work week would be Monday until Friday. Then, I would start this whole cycle over again in coming back home for the weekend. This drug that I was using would also keep me up all weekend. I was losing the chance to catch up on a decent amount of sleep. I was also stocking up on having enough to regularly do it throughout the work week. It wasn't long that I was once again hooked on an addictive substance that was affecting my life.

This time, it was not taking all of my money; I was making enough money where that was not a problem. Between the work week of using drugs all week and continuing this same habit even more intensely through the weekend, I had no chance to get regular sleep. This drug alone would affect my mental state in using heavy doses. To add little to no sleep with that skyrocketed my mental state being off in a matter of time. I got to the point where I once again became very paranoid. Once coming back to work after the weekend, I could tell that I was mentally off and that it was very noticeable to my work employees. As the week continued, I would slowly come back to my normal self as I drank myself to sleep during the nights.

That's how bad off that I became that I felt normal while drinking, and as long as I was only drinking, I was doing alright in my mind. I felt that was the only thing that gave me a personality. It would also calm me down from an intense high and help me get better sleep. After repeating this pattern of coming back from the weekend to work being extremely strung out, it was well-noticed and being talked about. There were even weeks where I was so out of it I demanded that I needed to go to the hospital. My company still worked with me and allowed me to have these requests and come back to work seeing that I was better off after some good sleep.

After continuing this bad cycle and not even realizing how ignorant that I was asking, they finally decided to drug test me. I was prepared for this, knowing that I was being noticed and had some fake urine warm and ready to use. I passed my drug test and they were surprised to see this, had nothing else to say, and let me go back to work. (They just thought I was crazy, which I am!)

After coming back from another weekend of using, I was in a whole 'nother galaxy at this point. I was so far gone in another mental breakdown that I thought that everything I was doing was a test. I was pretty much acting as Jim Carrey in *The Truman Show*. This is the best way that I can even explain how I was acting. Not that I have much memory of it but from what I do remember, that was literally on point how I was acting. I caused a big scene involving policemen, firemen, and an ambulance. They asked me what the problem was, I told them how I was thinking, and they took me to a hospital. I was taken to the ER, then later shipped from there to a detox facility. I was lucky to not have been taken to a mental hospital. I am thankful for that not being the case.

After getting some rest in there, and by rest I literally slept day to night for three to four days! After catching up on some rest, I came back to reality and my normal state of thinking. I realized how much of an idiot I had been and immediately switched from crazy mode to anxiety and panic mode. I wanted to know the situation with my job and how much longer they would keep me in this facility. I was also stranded in the next state over and wondered how I would even make it home. My brother, Sam, and a good family friend, Basil Diamond, came through for me and drove six hours to come get me. By this point, I was my happy self again and so happy just to be free from a place that gave me the feeling of being trapped; almost as if I was in jail. I was ordered by the doctors to stay there until their release and had multiple different interviews by different people working there, who analyzed my mental state to decide if I was ready to go back to the real world. After almost a week of staying there, they finally gave me permission and the consent to leave.

After being released, I found out that I no longer had a job. What a surprise that was! Just kidding! Thankfully, I made good money and had a few thousand dollars saved up. I realized that I had lost my journal from rehab and a lot of valuable tools. With knowing I no longer had a job and a decent amount of money, I decided to take advantage of the free time that I once again had. I went back to using heavy drugs daily again. I had no plan but was talking with my sister, and she gave me permission to stay with her as long as I abided by her rules. I agreed to do so and was thankful for the help that I was offered. I knew I was wanting to change, I also knew that I wanted to get more involved in the church. I knew that it would be fun living near the beach. I also knew that my sister and her husband are very successful. The pros outweighed the cons and this opportunity that I was given gave me hope that I could change once again in my life for the better!

> And now, my beloved brethren, after ye have gotten into this straight and narrow path, I would ask if all was done? Behold I say unto you, Nay; for ye have not come thus far save it were by the word of Christ with unshaken faith in him, relying wholly upon the merits of him who is mighty to save. Wherefore, ye must press forward with a steadfastness in Christ, having a perfect brightness of hope, and a love of God and of all men. Wherefore, if ye shall press forward, feasting upon the word of Christ, and endure to the end, behold, thus saith the Father: Ye shall have eternal life. (2 Nephi 31:19–20)

3

The Move to Florida

December 7, 2016

It has been an eventful year. A lot has happened to me and I feel compelled to share my story. Most of it has revolved around getting sober and building a closer relationship with God. I am trying to get my life back by focusing on these two main things that I feel are very important. It is nearly impossible to build a relationship with the Lord while under the influence.

In the beginning of this year, I knew that I needed help with some of the addictions that I had. They were destroying my life, taking everything that I had including my personality; the good in me that God gave me at birth. It was slowly being sucked out of me and practically turning me into a zombie struck dumb. My roommates saw my passions, abilities, and skills disappear. They directed and encouraged me to enter a six-month inpatient rehabilitation center.

That was one of the best decisions that I have made in my entire life. It didn't get me exactly where I needed to be, but it helped me tremendously to be in an inpatient program. There, I was able to receive positive support daily and finally realize that I'm not alone in this world in what I have been through. That I still have a chance! "God is our refuge and strength, a very present help in trouble." (Psalms 46:1).

December 11, 2016

Rehab didn't exactly do it for me. It did help me a lot but losing about ten years of my life is hard to recover from in a period of six months. Right now, I am currently staying with my sister, her husband, and three kids in Florida. I have very little of a plan made for myself but am putting my faith in them and Jesus Christ to help steer me in my next path of life. I am still waiting to see what will come next in following this path.

Like I said, I have very little plans that I have made, but here are the few goals that I have set for myself:

1. Run and do push-ups at least three times a week.
2. Write at least three pages a day in my journal.
3. Pray daily and read at least one chapter a day from *The Book of Mormon or Bible*.
4. Find some kind of steady work for myself.

There are more goals than these, but that is a start and what I am giving myself to actually put on paper. That is more than enough for me to accomplish for now. I give myself multiple goals all the time, normally, too many and slowly drop them one at a time. Actually, I guess I forgot a very major one that I should add, because I find it very important for myself to succeed: STAY SOBER! And that completes three pages of journal writing (actually four!), so I just completed some simple goals for myself. Go me!

December 12, 2016

I can't sleep but I feel obligated to write these goals down:

Ten Things That Will Change Your Life Forever

1. exercise twenty minutes daily
2. stretch twenty minutes daily
3. eat at least one healthy meal daily

4. switch your main source of drink to H20 (in time)
5. do something nice for somebody
6. do something nice for yourself
7. overly treat yourself once a week
8. overly treat someone else once a week
9. write one paragraph a day
10. read something inspirational ten minutes daily

December 13, 2016

Today, I got the opportunity to work. I worked with Richard Jenkins (a member in our ward at church). He is an electrician and does the same type of work that I have been trained in. I met his daughter. She was very sweet and has been through some of the same things that I have been through. I would love to be able to help her if she gave me the chance.

There is a lot on my mind right now. There is a lot that I have been through and want to fix in myself, as well as in others. I am thankful to be living with my sister Mary Kay and her husband, Tim. They are truly blessing me right now through the Lord. I am trying to understand how the Lord works and what He has in store for me. I am strongly thinking about serving a full-time mission for The Church of Jesus Christ of Latter-Day Saints for the Lord. There are still some things that I need to work on first though. For now, I am going to continue doing what I'm doing and keep my faith in Him.

December 14, 2016

Today, I was able to find more work with Brother Jenkins. It was a pretty good day. I also met with a counselor from the church. He suggested that I write some of my thoughts down. Little did he know that I had already started doing this again. My sister gave me this journal and said that I could have it if I start writing again. Well, I have been, and it is helpful.

Soon enough, I will write down some of my life stories and my thoughts that I shared with my counselor. For now, I am not ready to do that just yet. The thoughts alone have haunted me for years. I've already tried to write them down a couple of times and have gotten pretty far in the start of my story. Both times that I did, I ended up losing the journals that I wrote in. Sometimes, writing a story down keeps those thoughts circling in my brain even harder. It will drive me insane trying to write it as perfect as I think it. For now, I am happy sharing some of my thoughts with some people who care enough to hear it and not make me feel crazy for thinking that way. Another successful day!

The Decision to Fully Commit

December 18, 2016

Today was a very spiritual day. I had a good day at church. I had an even better night and made a decision that will probably change my life forever. It has been hitting me hard that it would be a wise decision to serve a mission. This means that I would be devoting two years of my life to the Lord and working in His footsteps. It is some-thing that I have wanted to do for a while; get closer to God.

What better way to do it than to serve Him for two years? This would entail a whole different style of how I'm used to living under His rules. This mindset is something I strongly need anyways, because I tend to make bad decisions when I am in the process of doing well. Any time that I start making positive changes in my life, it seems that I quickly slip away with bad mistakes.

There was a woman named Kimberly who I met today, who is interested in the gospel and meeting with the missionaries. She has a lot of things going on in her life and getting involved in church seems like the best option. I feel the same way.

It was comforting talking with her alongside the sister mission-aries, my sister, and brother-in-law. I felt the presence of the Spirit very strongly. It hit me hard that I want this more in my life.

I prayed at the end of our meeting and saw Kimberly burst into tears. Not negative tears but tears of comfort. The spirit was working in her as well as in me, telling us that the church is true. We have nothing to worry about if we come into His light. Feeling that peace and comfort is when I knew it is time to prepare to serve a mission for the Lord!

> And now, my son, I have told you this that ye may learn wisdom, that ye may learn of me that there is no other way or means whereby man can be saved, only in and through Christ. Behold, he is the life and the light of the world. Behold, he is the word of truth and righteousness. (Alma 38:9)

December 19, 2016

Today, some good things happened. I was led by the Spirit in paying tithing yesterday which is 10 percent of my income. The spirit told me that if I do this, then I will be blessed in receiving word about work. That gave me some faith that if I follow the Lord's commandments to the fullest, He will bless me with what I seek.

Because of that feeling I received, it gave me hope that sometime this week, I would receive word about getting a job. Miraculously, the very next day, I received a call back about a full-time job within walking distance of where I am staying! That tells me with confidence that heavenly Father is definitely real and does keep His promises with us as long as we do the same with Him. I'm really starting to get into this religion thing. It gets easier every day that I try. I pray that I may continue to do what I have been doing so I can prepare to be the best missionary of my ability. I hope that I may be able to prepare and increase my spirituality so that I may bless others with the gifts of God. I will help them see how He can make a difference in their lives too if they will just ask Him.

December 20, 2016

Today was another uplifting day. The days almost always stay positive when I am keeping my mind on the right path and doing what I'm supposed to be doing. I went to a twelve-step addiction recovery meeting with my newest best friend, Dustin. I know the Lord put him in my life for a reason. Other than Tim and Mary Kay, he has been one of the best people I could have in my life right now.

We are training to do a marathon, so by March, I hope to be prepared for that. It is always good to keep positive goals for myself. It keeps the body and mind occupied in continuous growth. Every negative has a positive; every positive brings more positives. I am going out with the missionaries tomorrow. I am both excited and curious to see where we will be going as well as who we will be teaching.

I hope that it will be a great experience and that I may be able to help add to their lessons. I am preparing to go on a mission myself soon, so now is the time to start preparing to serve God. "For behold, this life is the time for men to prepare to meet God; yea, behold the day of this life is the day for men to perform their labors" (Alma 34: 32).

December 25, 2016

"So this is Christmas. What a wonderful day! Another year older. A new one just begins" (Beatles). As I reflect on where I was one year ago at this time, I have grown so much in my life. Last Christmas, I was checked into a mental hospital after suffering a mental breakdown. I actually checked myself into the hospital. My mind wasn't all the way there, and I was struggling through some of the things that I had been doing.

Since then, I have made some major changes. I have committed to a week of sobriety and promised Jesus that this was my Christmas gift to Him.

> Yea, I would that ye would come forth and harden not your hearts any longer; for behold, now is the time and the day of your salvation; and therefore, if ye will repent and harden not your hearts, immediately shall the great plan of redemption be brought about unto you." -Alma 34:31

Amazingly I can now remember most of the events of this past year. I can look back at some of the major positive changes that I have made in my life and how much of a difference those changes helped me develop into who I am today.

Illustration by Dorthy Ledbetter

I can actually remember! That alone is a huge step. Looking back at last year, I can barely remember what even happened. There are pieces of the year but not many! Mostly, all that I recall is that

I finished the year in a hospital for my mental state. That is not a good place to be neither in body nor mind to finish a year. Now, I'm preparing to serve God! What a great change I have made from last year to this year.

"The Lord gives strength to his people; the LORD will bless his people with peace" (Psalm 29:11)!

December 30, 2016

Things have been going really well. I'm keeping up with my sobriety, as well as my positive habits and goals for myself. I met a man at church who is a recovered addict and alcoholic. He has been following up with me on my progress, making sure I'm staying sober. He has even asked my sister what her plan is when I fail.

He has been very real and honest with me, not to discourage me, but because of his experiences and how often he has seen people like me relapse. He told me that for a long time, he went to the weekly meetings himself, that every day he would wake up and say to himself, *Hi, I'm Kevin, I'm an alcoholic.* He finally decided he was tired of saying that every day and attending those weekly meetings indefinitely. He told me he had read a statistic somewhere that said around 98 percent of recovered addicts must attend weekly meetings and even identify themselves as an addict on a daily basis to avoid relapsing and going back to their old ways. Only a mere 2 percent can accomplish what I'm attempting to do: quit everything cold turkey and never go back again. He said he committed to be a part of that 2 percent, and so am I!

My schedule has gotten busier now that I have a full-time job, and because of that, it makes it harder for me to write every day. With that being the case, I believe that in order to make up for the days that I miss, I will take the time on weekends at least once a month, to put some hours into studying scriptures as well as writing in my journal. During that time of writing, I might focus more on some of my past stories and how they have formed me into who I am and the way that I think. (Most of my past stories are more negative things that I have done, but through those things, I have learned a lot.)

I know that one thing that I have is a passion for writing. I also enjoy reading, food, music, exercise, laughing, and learning. Right now, I am putting my time into learning about God. It is something I've put a lot of thought into but have never actually put my fullest energy into studying, living, or making it a lifestyle. I've been taught that God expects each of us humans to regularly do this in order to receive the fullest of His blessings.

I know it is one thing to think about but another to put my whole heart into what is expected of me. Therefore, I do not know God at all. All my thoughts mean nothing until I put all of my effort into what I know is expected. I cannot receive the blessings I know may be there until I do everything in my power to allow God to work His magic. I believe in magic! Do you?

I also know that all things are possible through Jesus Christ! And of all places in the universe for God to have sent His son to die for what we've done wrong, that makes us a very special breed of life if you ask me. We are created in GOD's IMAGE! This is either a very wicked planet and we are being punished, or a beautiful creation where we begin our knowledge. Whichever way you want to look at it.

Someone once told me that "the devil rules the mind, but God owns the heart!" The more that you allow God into your heart, the more He cleanses the mind. Something else that I was once told and am not positive of the accuracy of this statement, but I was once told that the heart has its own brain inside it as well. This is to make it work accordingly. All I know is that I am currently turning my heart over to God in the fullest. The more that I do this, the more peaceful, confident, knowledgeable, and happy I feel. I will so often receive tears of joy cleansing my mind of filthiness and telling my spirit that I will soon be a part of something miraculous. As will you if you allow the Lord to work in you as He has in me.

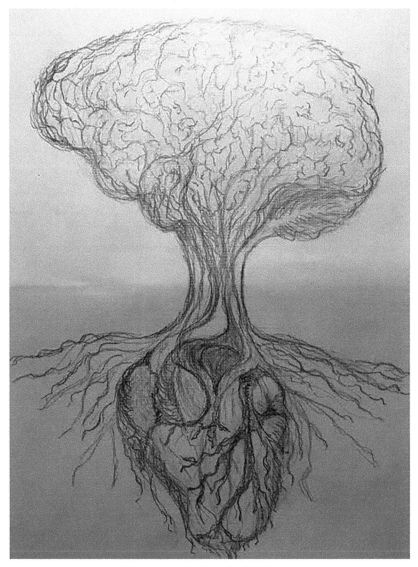

Illustration by Dorthy Ledbetter

January 1, 2017

It is a new year today. Today is the day where most people will set resolutions or goals for themselves that they want to accomplish throughout the year. This is something that I try to do for myself as well.

The difference between this year and my past is that this time, my heart feels strong. I feel healthier than normal. I also feel more alert, as well as more physically, mentally, and spiritually focused than I have ever been in my whole life. For the first time in my life, I feel like I will most likely accomplish the bar that I have set for myself. Normally, my bar is set too high, and I forget about it as the year goes on.

But this year, there are NO BLOCKS in the way of my path to stop me from the straight path that I am on! "Because straight is the gate, and narrow is the way, which leadeth unto life, and few there be that find it." (Matthew 7:14).

One of the blessings of keeping God and religion in my heart and mind is that it makes it nearly impossible for me to fall like I am used to doing.

And now, my sons, remember, remember that it is upon the rock of our Redeemer, who is Christ, the Son of God, that ye must build your foundation; that when the devil shall send forth his mighty winds, yea, his shafts in the whirlwind, yea, when all his hail and his mighty storm shall beat upon you, it shall have no power over you to drag you down to the gulf of misery and endless wo, because of the rock upon which ye are built, which is a sure foundation, a foundation whereon if men build they cannot fall. (Helaman 5:12)

Sobriety is key to this as well! So was changing my surrounding of people and having positive goals, which leads to POSITIVE ENERGY! (April Conference Talk Brighter Until a Perfect Day: "There is a tendency in all living systems toward positive energy [light] and away from negative energy [darkness]. From single-cell organisms to complex human systems, everything alive has an inherent inclination toward the positive and away from the negative.")

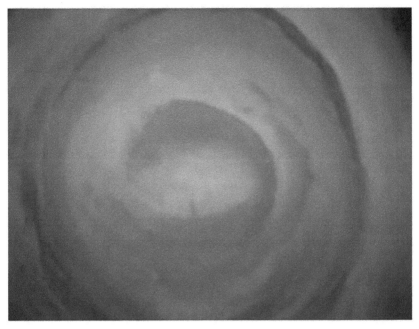

Illustration by Eliza Robinson

With that being said, here is what I have set for myself for the year 2017:

1. continue in scripture study daily
2. pray daily
3. write in journal weekly/daily if I can
4. run three to five times a week
5. upper body exercise three times weekly
6. vacation to the Florida Keys, hopefully in February
7. run a full marathon in March
8. buy a vehicle
9. go on a cruise
10. save a large percentage of my income
11. do everything that I can to prepare for my mission (physically, mentally, spiritually)
12. take a trip out of the country

January 8, 2017

Today is Fast Sunday. This is a special Sunday that my church does once a month. It is a day where we decide not to eat for twenty-four hours and normally have something or someone for whom we fast and pray. Doing so is very cleansing for the spirit and body, and a huge opportunity for spiritual growth. Also, the money that we would normally spend on those meals is given to the church where it is distributed to those that could use the help of food for their families.

This is a very spiritual day for our congregation. During our sacrament hour, we leave the microphone open to anyone bold enough to bear their testimony to the rest of the congregation. Normally, there are scheduled speakers with an assigned topic to speak on, given a prior notice to have that talk prepared. This is another part of what makes this Sunday so special. Fast Sunday has always been my favorite Sunday in our church!

You will feel the SPIRIT OF GOD there so strongly! The members of the congregation stand at the pulpit and speak spontaneously from the heart. "Blessed are the pure in heart, for they shall see God" (Matthew 5:8). Doing so, in my opinion, makes public speaking that much more POWERFUL. You are led by God in what to say, rather than our human thoughts in rationalizing how things are supposed to be said.

I bore my testimony today. This is something that I am wanting to grow as I prepare for my mission. There were a lot of thoughts and things that I wanted to say beforehand. This is something nearly impossible to do, whenever being filled with the spirit. Even though I did not get all of my points across, I got the main point across that I wanted to say. Just barely, while also getting emotional in the process of speaking and running off the stand. I told everyone that I love them! I also told them that there is mainly one problem I have had: one thing inside me that has been holding me back and halting my progression.

While focusing on and correcting this problem, it has made everything in my life so much easier. By committing to sobriety, it has given me my life back. I finally get to be me again! I am logically thinking again in a positive manner. I am remembering who I was when I was younger, back when I was naturally happy. The feeling that I can do anything in this world is back! That feeling of hope is back. That person that was in me this whole time, that I thought was lost over the years. I am once again my old self.

Not only my old self, but a more mature, wiser version of myself. Therefore, I am now the exact person I need to be in this time and age, ready to take on any challenge that comes my way.

This was the main point of my testimony, and hopefully, this message was received well. Perhaps I am mistaken, but I believe that there is one major thing that each individual should change for themselves. If only they knew how to conquer the struggle inside themselves that is empowering them and keeping them down. If they were mentally capable in doing so, their whole lives could drastically change forever.

All they have to do is reverse that one blockage that is planted in their mind. Or pick it out of their brain altogether, whichever the case may be. I believe that this world—our world, our people, are capable of so much with so much understanding and knowledge that we all have. Just think of all the possibilities! If we all worked together as the family that we all are. As a team! All on the same team. Not competing against each other with the best houses, cars, or careers. Not trying to one up each other all the time or put each other down but working together as a UNITY. There is so little being done because we cannot even help ourselves. When in reality, it is probably only one simple solution that we each need to do, in order to make the change necessary to be happy.

I am an electrician, so I will put that in electrical terms for you, or for you kids in elementary terms. It is as simple as an ON/OFF switch. Let me rephrase that through the addiction recovery that I have received. This is actually the very first step to addiction recovery. I can tell you from experience that it seems so simple but is actually the hardest step: ADMITTING YOU HAVE A PROBLEM!

I know that change is hard and can even be scary. It is so easy to stay exactly where you are at! We are comfortable, right? Happy, yes? Our family is fine exactly the way it is, is it not? I am only one opinion, one voice, but I say wrong!

Here is something about myself: I have a good or positive sense of energy or emotion, which in my opinion makes me a good judge of character or people. This has also been my greatest blessing and curse at the same time. I seem to sense people's spirit (what is inside them) and pull out the good that I know everybody has. Yes, I said it, there is good in EVERYBODY! Fact! I have met too many people in my life and know this to be true. And the types of different people that I have met that range and vary in so many different ways; it is too hard to explain or write down on paper.

The downside, however, is that along with the good everybody has, there is also bad! (Good=God/Bad=Devil) "Submit yourselves therefore to God. Resist the devil, and he will flee from you. Draw nigh to God, and he will draw nigh to you. Cleanse your hands, ye sinners; and purify your hearts, ye double minded" (James 7:4–8). People that focus on the bad tend to be more negative. Even with the good side that person has, the bad will tend to overrule, leaving them in an intense and more aggressive state of mind. Also, having that mindset will tend to make them take advantage of whoever they can, believing that it will make their lives easier. Those people take kindness as a weakness. I try to be kind therefore in of lot of eyes I am weak, as well as an easy target.

E=MC2 OR ENERGY: MIRROR SEES TWO

Illustration by Christian Probst

This is an endless cycle these types will prey on. Some of them change or get out of that cycle like I choose to do or keep the cycle going. This goes for both categories, and I have played both roles in this aspect (predator/prey). Acting the way that I do has given me a lot of downfalls in my life. Not because of me being kind. It is because of who I am and how I was raised and what I was expected to do. While under the influence, I was not in my right mind which made me weak. I was often in a delirious state and a lesser version of myself. Therefore, I was not the best me that inside, I knew I could be.

Illustration by Christian Probst

Do I regret those trials? Not at all! It is because of those experiences that I have been through that has formed and molded me into the person that I am today. I am no longer doing those things that held me back in life. Therefore, I am STRONG!

And if men come unto me I will show unto them their weakness. I give unto men weakness that they may be humble; and my grace is sufficient for all men that humble themselves before me; for if they humble themselves before me, and have faith in me, then will I make weak things become strong unto them. (Ether 12:27)

Like I said before, there was only one flaw, one downfall, one problem that I had. There was only one thing inside me that I needed to change about myself, that would drastically change my life forever. Everything that I just talked about is what I would have wanted to share in my testimony but of course, could not go into that much detail.

At least, with the few sentences I did say before the congregation, that was the main point I was trying to make while bearing my testimony. Practice is how you strengthen something. So here are the three points I bore in my testimony today as far as I recall:

1. I want to strengthen my testimony, so this is how I do it.
2. There has only been one problem holding me back in life.
3. I was overcome with emotion from the spirit I felt and closed saying, "I love you."

I feel emptiness inside everybody, even those that have a wonderful life. I know somewhere deep inside everyone, there is one simple fix we can each resolve that will make all the difference in the world. Not "the world" but OUR WORLD! Even though I explained this in writing, those three points were practically what my testimony consisted of and said on the stand. I received a lot of thank yous after and pray that each person there will change whatever it is inside them that is holding them back from progression. As well as conquering it and receiving eternal happiness to the fullest! "Lord, thou hast been our dwelling place in all generations. Before the mountains were brought forth, or ever thou hadst formed the earth and the world, even from everlasting to everlasting, thou art God" (Psalms 90:1–2).

January 15, 2017

Today is Sunday again. This is the main day that I plan to write from this point forward. It is the Sabbath Day, the day that we go to church, as well as the day that we remember the Lord to the fullest. I figure, what a better day to write than when the spirit has revolved around me the most. I know at one point, I was wanting to write every day. This has changed since getting a job. It has changed my schedule where I decided to write weekly. I also did not want to keep writing the same things over daily. I wanted this writing to be more meaningful!

Besides that change, I am still continuing all the other goals that I have made for myself, including sobriety! Of all the goals that I have made, I find scripture study to be the most important of those goals. I feel that studying and pondering the scriptures gives me a closer relationship with my heavenly Father. It will help my relationship continue to grow as well. Scripture study is the newest of goals that I have made for myself. In my past, I never really saw the importance of it. As I continue to read them and study daily, I am beginning to see why this is a commandment. These records were written for a reason by ancient prophets and preserved for our day, so that each of us can read in these modern days. This is the Earth's history of life and important to know why we are even here. That reason is to help us grow spiritually and to prepare to meet God. "And all flesh shall see the salvation of God" (Luke 3:6).

There are other commandments as well that the Lord expects of us. I do not understand fully why our heavenly Father gives us the commandments that He does. "And after many days an angel of the Lord appeared unto Adam, saying: 'Why dost thou offer sacrifices unto the Lord?' And Adam said unto him: 'I know not, save the Lord commanded me'" (Moses 5:6). I also do not understand why people have the trials that they do, while some people suffer greater than others. To be honest, there are a lot of things that I question and want to understand.

This is where I believe FAITH comes in. Even with all the things that I do not know, I do know this: Everything in life happens for a reason. Every decision that I make becomes a factor in what happens next in my life. I am currently using what religion calls FAITH! Not only faith, but faith in God! As far as I am concerned, this is the most powerful force in the universe to have. I also believe this to be a percentage of brain power that our minds are not using. LACK OF FAITH! It is one thing to say that you believe in something and another to actually do it.

I know that once I decided to put my devotion in this church to the fullest, I have seen no downside to it. I find my confidence boosting daily! I find myself constantly happy! I find myself setting positive goals for myself and actually accomplishing them!

I find myself to be more alert, diligent, and focused than I have ever been in my entire life! I am finding growth in myself and am seeing this happen in others as well!

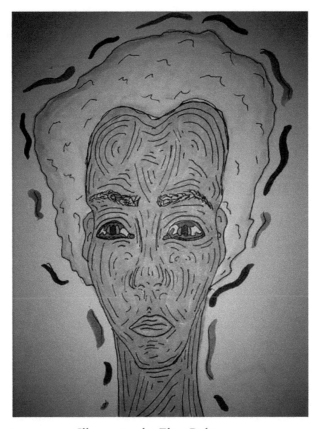

Illustration by Eliza Robinson

I am somebody that recognizes these gifts to be BLESSINGS FROM GOD! I know them to be real and true. They are uplifting, clean, and positive feelings. I see them to be continuing and plenty more to come as long as I do what I am expected to do from the Lord. I recognize them to be the beginning of no end. As long as I keep my faith in Him, I will be poured upon with His blessings, as will you. "Prove me now herewith, saith the Lord of Hosts, if I will not open you the windows of heaven, and pour you out a blessing, that there shall not be room enough to receive it" (Malachi 3:10).

These blessings are what is said to be a natural high or eternal bliss. I remember in one part of my life a comment that my father would regularly say to me: "Ignorance is bliss!" I pondered on this statement for years. What does this mean? Sometimes, my father would give me a hard time if I questioned some of his statements. Rather than feeling talked down upon, I would just pretend like I knew what he was trying to tell me.

I still wondered though, what does this statement mean? I do not have the best vocabulary. I know what ignorance means, but it was that word bliss that was throwing me off. Not a common word used in modern day vocabulary. Ignorance means stupid right? But what about bliss? I thought about this statement for years. One day, I had this phrase on my mind. I ended up asking a good friend, knowing that his vocabulary was advanced. He told me that bliss means happiness. I could not help but to smile. WOW! This was all that I could think. He was right because I tend to be a mostly happy person. I also look at the birds in the sky, and what I would give to be in the sky with them right now.

Illustration by Christian Probst

Another statement I enjoy is "Knowledge is power!" Our time and people have plenty of this. How many things we could do if we used this in a positive manner and put it to good use.

> But as it written, eye hath not seen, nor ear heard, neither have entered into the heart of man, the things which God hath prepared for

them that love Him. But God hath revealed them
unto us by His Spirit: for the Spirit searcheth all
things, yea, the deep things of God. For what
man knoweth the things of a man, save the spirit
of man which is in Him? Even so the things of
God knoweth no man, but the Spirit of God. (1
Corinthians 2:9–11)

"Knowledge is power." I remember learning a song in elementary school that consisted of these words. It is crazy how much we
learn at such a young age. "Music the great communicator; music is
my aeroplane" (Anthony Kiedis)!

I am not sure a hundred percent on these statistics, but I believe
it to be like 70 percent of our knowledge and learning happens by the
time that we are eight. I have also been taught that we use only 20
percent of our brain. And this is being courteous. This is compared
to more of an advanced mind like Stephen Hawking. These numbers
may not completely add up, but I believe my percentage to be some-
what accurate. I mean think about it! From childbirth, we learn to
crawl, talk, walk, read, write, etc. The list goes on. There is so much
that we learn at such a young age. Think of how we could teach our
children if we taught them what they are capable of at a young age.
How can we train our kids to properly grow?

It amazes me how many biblical stories that I already know
from childhood, as I am reading them again in my scripture study as
an adult. It is a pretty cool experience learning this as I reread these
stories that I already know. I guess I do not have to start from scratch
like I thought that I did.

Well, this pretty much sums up all that I have for this week. I
am very satisfied with the progress that I have made for myself this
year. This truly began when my sister, Mary Kay, and brother-in-law,
Tim, allowed me into their home. It helped increase my spiritual
growth for myself when I saw the happiness and success that God has
given them. My own progression started when I took religion into
my heart to the fullest. This happened when I decided for myself that
I wanted to change my surroundings and lifestyle. I have seen some

very positive results since I have done this and believe to see many more blessings to come in my near future. "The Lord is righteous in all His ways, and holy in all His works. The Lord is nigh unto all them that call upon him, to all that call upon him in truth" (Psalms 145:17–18).

I also wanted to make this a positive week of writing because next week, I think I will be ready to start writing about my past. There will definitely be more negative things written there. I believe this is why I have waited so long to begin writing about them. There are some real sensitive subjects that have happened in my life. These incidents have molded me into who I am today. Because of this, I do not only see it as a bad experience, but a learning experience. I have said this before and will say it again, being a strong believer in this statement: "Every negative has a positive, but every positive does not always have a negative; nothing but more positives!"

> And in that day, thou shalt say: O Lord, I will praise thee; though thou wast angry with me thine anger is turned away, and thou comfortedst me. Behold, God is my salvation; I will trust, and not be afraid; for the Lord Jehovah is my strength and my song; He also has become my salvation. Therefore, with joy shall ye draw water out of the wells of salvation. And in that day shall ye say: Praise the Lord, call upon His name, declare His doings among the people, make mention that His name is exalted. Sing unto the Lord; for He hath done excellent things; this is known in all the earth. Cry out and shout, thou inhabitant onion; for great is the Holy One of Israel in the midst of thee. (2 Nephi: 22)
>
> God gives some of his GREATEST CHALLENGES to his GREATEST WARRIORS!

The Story of My Life

February 16, 2017

Today is Thursday. It has been a good year so far. Last time that I wrote, I said that I was going to write down some of my past. I believe this to be the reason I have taken so long to continue my writing. I am more of a present/future kind of person.

Illustration by Caleb Larkins

Right now, I am camping on an island down in the Keys of Florida. I came down here with two of my more recent church friends, Kelly, and his son, Christian. So, I thought, what a great time and place to do some writing. This makes me feel as the prophet John, when he was writing Revelations. This initially is what the scriptures are: people's journals being made into records of history.

I will start from the very beginning of my history. I was born on August 9, 1991, in Vanderbilt Hospital of Nashville, Tennessee; the sixth child of James and Dorthy Hebda. My mother was raised in Alabama while my father was from Pennsylvania, both from large families themselves. They met in college at Brigham Young University in Provo, Utah, and eventually settled in Clarksville, Tennessee, where he was a licensed psychologist. As I share my history, you will see why my six siblings and I formed a close bond, enduring the same challenges and upbringing together. My oldest brother, Johnny, is ten years older than me; followed by my only sister, Mary Kay; then brothers, Jimmy, Sam, and Adam; me, then the youngest brother, Joe. We are all two years apart and the four youngest brothers are especially close.

Now is where I start the history of my past life. Where do I even start, when I am already twenty-five years old? I suppose as far back as I can remember. The first major incident that I recall happened to me when I was five. This happened when I first received my knowledge of riding a bicycle. First step to riding a bike: learn how to balance and pedal without training wheels. And that is pretty much all that it requires to learn this skill. I accomplished this task and was enjoying it very much.

During this time, I wanted to go faster. I found a steep hill on my parent's property. This looked like a good opportunity to make that happen. I went down the hill. I started going faster than expected. I wanted to slow down. I forgot how to use the brakes. Or maybe this was an important second step to riding a bike that I had forgotten about. I thought, *Oh no, what do I do?* Guess I did not fully learn to ride a bicycle yet like I had thought! My head hit a tree on impact. I had now slowed down, actually stopped. This tree probably left a golf-ball-sized knot on my head.

My father was very angry about this, not the reaction you would expect from a parent when I was injured. I lost my bicycle privileges for some time. From that point on, my dad targeted me in scripture study as well as other learning skills. I did not understand why. As I got older, I began to think about why he had cared so much. Part of this was him being mentally ill himself. Also, he is a psychologist and recognized this head injury I had received at such a young age. He knew this would most likely cause permanent brain damage for me, the remainder of my life. This is the first painful memory I can remember from a young age.

It also seemed like I was born to rebel against my teachings of the gospel at an early age. I was still a kind person but liked to act the opposite of what I was taught to be right. I believe a lot of this was to seem cool or fit in at school. That is probably one explanation but not the only reason for my actions. I also believe this was just part of who I was born to be, as well as what I liked to do. I enjoyed pleasure! Therefore, I enjoyed things that made me laugh or feel good. I remember even from a young age inappropriately touching myself because of the pleasure that it gave me. For the longest time, I thought this to be abnormal. I did not understand why I made these actions, so from a young age, viewed myself as different. I almost felt as if I were an animal and was afraid to even discuss these feelings because of how I thought others might view me.

I also remember using bad language and curse words as young as elementary school. This seemed to be the way to be cool, even at that age. I already had a mindset for public society and the way to fit in with who seemed to be cool, and that was by being bad. This seemed to be important to how these kids viewed me; therefore, I learned to be a rebel as far back as early grade school.

Another incident I remember from early elementary school is another painful memory. It was an incident with my father. Having a large family made it rare for me to be left alone with my dad. He has regular mood swings and is diagnosed as bipolar. This gave me great anxiety if ever I was left alone with him, without the support of another family member.

One day, after a bath, I found this to have happened. I'm still not really sure where the rest of the family went. He yelled my name in anger as I was getting dressed. Apparently, he went into my room while I was taking a bath. The room was not up to his standards, therefore, messy, and this made him angry. I remember him having a belt. He beat me black-and-blue on the stairs that led to my room. This was not the first time he had physically abused me or my siblings.

My mom was ready to leave him after this incident because of his actions. She left the decision up to me. He promised he would not hit us anymore. He felt very sorry and bought me some toys. He also let me stay home from school for some days. (Although it probably had more to do with letting my bruises heal before going back.) I forgave him! For the most part, he kept his promise and never really hit any of us ever again. However, he still had regular mood swings, was angry a lot, and was very verbally abusive. It seemed that by stopping the physical abuse, that only increased the verbal mistreatment. These actions did not stop the remainder of my childhood.

Even though this was his personality about seventy percent of the time, the other thirty percent of him was very loving. While in his happy moods, he could be one of the most loving and caring people that I have ever met. He also has a better understanding of life, as well as religion than the average person. His memory is one of the best I have ever seen, in areas that he chose to use it in. It seemed he could quote hundreds of scriptures off the top of his head. When it came to bad memories, he seemed to block them out and pretend as if certain events did not happen. If only he practiced what he preached! Actions speak louder than words. He would often quote, "Smart people learn from their mistakes. Wise people learn from others' mistakes." Too bad he rarely followed his own advice! He has many symptoms of not being mentally stable even while in a good mood. He often became overly nice while happy, even to the point where driving to get fast food or going to other public places, people would sometimes question if he was under the influence.

What goes up, must come down! I noticed this pattern in him throughout the years: happy, angry, sad, depressed. A constant cycle that happened with him regularly throughout the weeks. He could not carry a stable mood, even if he tried. What makes this even more ridiculous is the fact that as a licensed psychologist, he was the person that other people would go to for psychological help. Or maybe, this is a perfect explanation for his actions, always having to hear other people's problems.

My mother had a very stable mood, as far as I was concerned. She was a stay-at-home mom, that took care of the house and was the peacemaker for the family. During her free time of not being too busy with family duties as a mom, she enjoyed arts and crafts and gardening as her hobbies. She is a very artistic individual who is very blessed in these areas. By arts and crafts, I do not mean your basic papier-maché crafting. She is a little more advanced than this. Just two skills off the top of my head that she developed were stained glass and welding. There are other skills she has to go with that. She is very good with her hands and very unique compared to other moms that I have been around. She is also one of the most caring and loving people that I have ever met. I am blessed to have the mom that I do and could not have asked for a better role model of how a mother should be.

My only regret from her is her motherly instinct of always wanting to make peace. She gave in to please my father when he was in the wrong. I know this may be hard for some women, being the gentle, caring, breeds of life they are designed to be, but it is important to be strong daughters of Zion! Especially when there are things happening in your home negatively affecting yourself but even more importantly, if they are negatively affecting your children.

"Let your conversation be without covetousness; and be content with such things as ye have: for he hath said, I will never leave thee, nor forsake thee" (Hebrews 13:5).

These are some thoughts that I have for both of my parents. Even with the unstable home I was raised in, I am blessed to have the two loving, intelligent parents that I have. Even through the chaos, my parents did a great job of teaching my family love, the importance of religion, and the difference of right and wrong. (Even if a lot of this was learned by observing their actions and how NOT to raise a family or build a relationship.)

With that being said, back to some memories I have from my childhood. As far back as late elementary school and all throughout middle, even early high school, my friends and I got into vandalism whenever we had the chance. I do not think this was something I did for popularity. I believe the reason for doing this (as well as many younger kids do to this day) was to cope with how I felt on the inside. This seemed to make me happy, destroying other people's possessions. I was fortunate to have only gotten caught a few times. Otherwise, I would have had a much larger background record than I already have. I even remember one of my best friends getting in major trouble over something that we regularly did. This was something that followed him, and he had to deal with for multiple years. That was a red flag for me, that I needed to stop what I was doing.

Another thing I greatly remember is learning about pornography. This happened in early middle school. I found out that I was not the only one and that other people did what I did in secret. This was a huge surprise to me. I still did not feel comfortable talking about this subject (it was a sensitive topic) but remember it severely helping me to reconcile with what I thought made me abnormal, even insane. I remember this being a huge relief. I was not alone! I was not as different as I thought I was. I had those feelings for many of years.

> Thou art my hiding place; thou shalt preserve me from trouble; thou shalt compass me about with songs of deliverance. I will instruct thee and teach thee in the way which thou shalt go: I will guide thee with mine eye. Be ye not as the horse, or as the mule, which have no understanding: whose mouth must be held in with bit and bridle, lest they come near unto thee. Many sorrows shall be to the wicked: but he that trusteth in the Lord, mercy shall compass him about. (Psalms 32:7–10)

I remember my father talking about his past regularly throughout my life. How bad he was as an adolescent, until he found The Church of Jesus Christ of Latter-Day Saints. While talking about these stories, he would regularly brag on himself, as well as how much "fun" he had while under the influence. My advice to you is: DO NOT TELL YOUR KIDS STORIES LIKE THIS! If you do, definitely do not go into detail or base these stories into how much fun you were having. I am a curious person, and you say something is fun, I want to know why. I can tell you from experience that all drugs or alcohol do is take over your life and prevent you from skills and talents that you are capable of achieving. It will block you from your abilities to strengthen the best version of who you are. It will keep you from your blessings you are born here to receive in this life and let grow.

To go with this subject will lead to my next line of stories. It has been great meditation and very therapeutic to have put some of these memories on paper. I have been procrastinating some of my painful memories for a very long time. I can see why I have felt the desire to write some of these memories down. The feeling of relief I have felt doing this, I cannot even put into words. I can say in confidence that this has been the most exciting project I have ever given myself. The mysteries of GOD unfold in my life every day. Right before my eyes! The joy He gives me, as I do a work for Him! I feel His LOVE in me! This is a feeling I will once again say, that NO WORDS can explain! "He that sitteth in the heavens shall laugh: The Lord shall have them in derision. Be wise now therefore, O ye kings: be instructed, ye judges of the earth" (1 Peter 2:4 and 10).

Anyways, I am currently on vacation! Time to explore more of the Caribbean and hopefully catch some lobster!

Illustration by Caleb Larkins

Thoughts Are Things
Author Unknown

I hold it true that thoughts are things;
They are endowed with bodies and breath and wings;
And that we send them forth to fill.
The world with good results, or ill.
That which we call our secret thought.
Speeds forth to Earth's remotest spot.
Leaving its blessings or its woes

Like tracks behind it as it goes.
We build our future, thought by thought,
For good or ill, yet know it not
Yet, so "The Universe" was wrought.
Thought is another name for fate;
Choose, then, thy destiny and wait.
For love brings love and hate brings hate.
A human face I love to view
And trace the passions of the soul;
On it the spirit writes a new.
Each thought and feeling on a scroll.
There the mind its evil doings tells,
And there its noblest deeds to speak;
Just as the ringing of the bells
Proclaims a knell or wedding feast.

February 26, 2017

That was a poem I really enjoyed. I will normally write something down if it stands out to me. It came from a book that my bishop asked me to read called *The Miracles of Forgiveness* written by Spencer W. Kimball. This was a step of my repentance process of receiving forgiveness from the Lord. There are many different ways to repent. My bishop asked me to make this one of my steps of repentance. He is my bishop, therefore, represents the Lord, so I figured it would be in my best interest to obey his orders. This will also give me forgiveness to the fullest.

And it came to pass that I, Nephi, said unto my father: "I will go and do the things which the Lord hath commanded, for I know that the Lord giveth no commandments unto the children of men, save he shall prepare a way for them that they may accomplish the thing which he commandeth them." (1 Nephi 3:7)

I am now back from my vacation to the Keys. After the time we spent together traveling, Kelly and his son, Christian, are now two of my best friends here. It was a great experience and actually one of the coolest things that I have ever done. We took kayaks out to a small island down there and camped under the stars for a couple of nights. During that time, we caught fresh lobster, crab, and fish to eat. That is what Kelly does for a living. He studied marine biology and specializes in selling freshly caught fish. That is how he markets his product with having a new shipment of different fish caught weekly. This is what these amazing chefs want because of how much different they taste when fresh. Fish do not taste the same when stored frozen for weeks. I can now personally say this to be true. One of my main goals of our trip was to be able to snorkel and spear at least one lobster on my own. I might have mentioned this earlier. As a group, I believe we ended up catching fifty-one lobsters. Successful trip! I believe that goal was met.

These are fun experiences I plan to do more often. It is more likely to happen now that I am no longer enslaved to my addictions. I now have a lot more free time to do as I want. The weird part is, I'm probably busier than I have been in my whole life, and still find that last statement to be true!

> I am the vine, ye are the branches: He that abideth in me, and I in him, the same bringeth forth much fruit: for without me ye can do nothing. Henceforth, I call you not servants; for the servant knoweth not what his lord doeth: but I have called you friends; for all things that I have heard of my Father I have made known unto you. (John 15:5 and 15)

Today, I also met with my stake president to see if I am eligible to leave for my mission. They have rules on whether an individual qualifies or is allowed to serve for this kind of mission. He is not 100 percent certain yet if I am going to be allowed to serve and is waiting to hear back from a higher authority. That kind of crushed my spirit when he told me this news. I almost wanted to give up on the progress that I made and go back to my old ways. It would be silly to do that now, after everything that I have done to improve and strengthen myself.

I decided that I am not going to do that! I would only be hurting myself! I would also be hurting my family as well as anybody else that believes in me. That would be selfish of me to hurt them again, after they have just started to heal from the pain I left them over the years.

I also remember the promise I made to Jesus Christ, one week before Christmas. I made a covenant with Him that I would not go back to my old ways and commit to sobriety for him. A simple promise to keep after all of the sacrifices He has made for me. My KING! My eternal brother that I will pray to for all eternity! "The Lord is my rock, and my fortress, and my deliverer; my God, my strength, in whom I will trust; my buckler, and the horn of my salvation, and my high tower. I will call upon the Lord, who is worthy to be praised: so shall I be saved from mine enemies" (Psalm 18:2–3).

These were some of the more recent things that have happened in my life that I thought I should write down. Even though I heard the news that I may not be able to serve a mission, we finished our meeting with a prayer. It was a very powerful blessing that I had asked to receive. It was a blessing to me through President Larsen directly from GOD! It said some great things. Most importantly, I was told that I am forgiven! GOD directly told me that He forgives me! There were many other great things said as well, too much to put into writing. I remember as I was receiving the blessing, my stake president's tone of voice changing, as well as his words speeding up, as he started speaking of Isaiah. There was such a powerful spirit in the room! By the end of it, we were all crying with tears of joy. My brother-in-law, Tim, was there as well. President Larsen had asked him to join us for my blessing. That helped me feel a lot better at the end of my interview.

Even with the bad news, that blessing made up for it. The most comforting part of the whole blessing was hearing that God and Jesus Christ had both forgiven me. This is pretty much all that I have for now. Next time that I write, I will finish up my story of my past. My adolescent years, when there were pretty much only three things on my mind: girls, drugs, and alcohol!

February 28, 2017

Today is the last day of February. I moved here at the end of November. The day after Thanksgiving to be exact. I have accomplished a lot in three months. I must always remember this. There is a positive spirit that lifts me up from conquering everything that slowed me down. Today is also a Tuesday. I missed work today. I will explain why I missed work later (I do not randomly miss work unless there is a reason). For now, I need to finish the story of my life. It means a lot to me to write this down. It shows how I was raised, my actions growing up, and where I am at right now in my life. "I will love thee, O Lord, my strength" (Psalm 18:1).

I believe I was in middle school where I had last written of my past. This is where I started experimenting and abusing drugs and alcohol. I am not exactly sure what brought me to this level of going down this path. As far as I can remember, it is just from being the curious person that I am and wanting to understand why people talk about, do, or even enjoy some of these bad habits. The very first thing that I ever remember abusing was cough syrup. I had gotten the idea from watching *South Park*. That was the start of a long journey of trial and error I began for myself.

Be careful what shows you allow your children to watch for that reason. My parents were definitely against these kinds of shows. I suppose that we were not well enough supervised during some of the times we watched TV. Nowadays, they have filters to block out inappropriate shows. This should eliminate that problem. Soon after experimenting the cough syrup incident, I found out that my next-door neighbor was just as curious as I was in these areas. I'm not even sure how the conversation was brought up, but I remember being both surprised and happy at the same time to hear that he was thinking along the same lines that I was. According to what my parents, school, and church taught, drugs and alcohol are harmful and not something to mess with. For this reason, I did not talk about it in fear of getting in trouble.

As soon as my best friend/neighbor brought this subject up, it made me that much more comfortable, therefore, easier to participate in these actions. This also gave me a friend to discuss these thoughts with of what might be fun to try next (misery loves company). At this time, it was not misery. It was what we called fun, experimenting, and being free spirits! It did not become a problem as far as I was concerned until years down the road. I mean all that it was affecting was all of my free time spent on partying, my progression in sports, my grades, my memory, and my brain cells. That was it! Nothing too serious, right? Okay, so now my best friend who was also my next-door neighbor wants to experience in being under the influence, as well as myself. This pretty much now became the focus of conversation for me and my friends from that point on pretty much for the rest of my life.

Me: So you like drugs and alcohol?"
Friend: Yes.
Me: Cool, me too! What do you want to do?"
Friend: Do you know anybody who sells weed?
Me: No!
Friend: Me neither or money, but my mom has box wine! We can get drunk!"

So that is what we did. We each got a red disposable party cup, filled it up with box wine out of my neighbor's garage, and walked out back near the woods to drink it. We both took a sip, realized how terrible that it tasted, so both of us chugged our glasses real quick. That way, we no longer had to have that terrible taste in our mouths. This was the second time that I was ever under the influence. This was now the friendship that we had; best friends under the influence. It lasted about three to four years until we stopped regularly hanging out. Both his and my parents got tired of us always getting into trouble to the point that I was no longer allowed at his house. According to his parents, I was the bad influence and it was my fault for the things that we did. The friendship that we had of hanging out daily lasted from grades seven to nine.

Another thing that it seemed like from the school we went to or at least according to the crowd that we hung out with, was that my friend and I were some of the first people in our group to be experimenting in these kinds of ways. This made us bad influences. These influences slowly grew as we went through high school and even more after high school. There were people in school that were straight-A students, as well as in honor classes that fell down this path soon after being out of high school. These were people that I never imagined seeing these kinds of things happening to. In some ways, that could be an even worse age to start going down that path.

I was one who started young with substance abuse, which was middle school. Like I said, young according to my friends. Nowadays and even when I was younger, there are people that go through these stages in early elementary school. With starting this in middle school, my high school partying became even worse (and as an adult became just absurd, but I'll get to some of those details later). In high school, I was using things as a freshman that people to this day would never dare to try. If they did decide to experiment in these ways, it normally was not until college or years after that.

This gave me a bad reputation, and I had multiple friends' parents who did not allow me into their homes. I was known as the bad influence between my friends' parents. Looking back at it, my friends probably had gotten into trouble over something and blamed that fault on me. This would release the tension and burden from it falling only on them. This is how kids are, nobody likes being in trouble with their parents at that age.

They are the ones who control your freedom in what you can and cannot do. By the time I was a sophomore, I found it very difficult to remember stuff inside and outside of school. My memory was bad enough as it was.

I did not need supplements to decrease that even more. I found it very difficult to do schoolwork and was failing some of my classes. I realized then the damage that it was causing but still continued to ignore those thoughts, because my passion for partying was too great. Therefore, it overruled my health.

I was also a wrestler. I began in the sixth grade. By the time I was a freshman, I was pretty good. That was the only thing that kept me as functional as I was. I was varsity level on a pretty good team. We placed in state all four years that I was in school, as well as plenty of years prior to me coming there. My freshman year, we lost the state championship by only one point! I lost my match so blame myself for not winning a state championship. If I hadn't partied so much, I most likely would have won that match.

I figured I still had three more years to make up for it. We never came that close to winning though, only placed third or fourth. I didn't realize how good of a team that we had my freshman year. Wrestling has two state tournaments: individual and team. I came pretty close to placing almost every year. My sophomore year was my closest. I lost in double overtime which kept me from placing. I beat myself up so much over that loss, and to top it off, my coach was as upset as I was about losing.

He came up to me afterward and said, "That's what you get for being a dang hippie! How about you not party so hard this next summer!"

I was so torn up, I cried in the hallway for a bit. Same with my team after we lost the state finals. We held the team state tournament at my school, so after we lost, we had to deal with the other team celebrating and prancing around our school. I have never been in a room of some of the toughest people that I have ever met, all crying together.

We had such a strong team and coach, Jeff Jordan. He was what made our team. He is a big part of who molded me into who I am today, being the great coach that he was. He always lifted weights with us three times a week, even being in his fifties. There are not too many coaches that would do that. I have tremendous respect for him. I didn't finish as well as I wanted to, but at the end of the season of my senior year, I thanked him (while being a little tearful) for being the great coach that he was.

Another significant event that happened during my freshman year was that our house got hit by a tornado. To make it even more ironic, my mom's name is Dorthy, like *The Wizard of Oz*! I know sometimes that I write things out of order, but that is how my brain operates. I'm very ADHD which made it very hard to concentrate in school. On the positive side of that is that I am very good at multi-tasking. So I was put on Adderall at a young age. As I got older, I realized that it is also a drug and that I could abuse it and get high from it. I liked how it felt if I upped the milligrams on it and took a large amount. I guess you could say I have a very addictive personality. I found that other people in school liked them as well, so I could even sell them if I wanted to, which I occasionally did.

Illustration by my mother, Dorthy Ledbetter

After my house was hit by the tornado, we stayed in hotels for a few weeks. Then we stayed in a rental house while they finished rebuilding and repairing the damage to our home. If I remember correctly, we stayed in the rental house for most of my high school experience. I think it was at the end of my junior year or beginning of my senior year that we moved back into the house. During this time, my older brother and some of our friends realized that the property that was down in the woods by our wrecked house was the perfect spot for partying. There were also plenty of trees knocked over that needed to be burned which allowed plenty of firewood for bonfires. That place was a wreck, symbolic of our lives and how we all felt inside. My friends and my family, torn apart inside, pretending like everything was okay.

Every weekend starting early Saturday mornings, we were expected to work. This was expected of us both before and after the tornado happened. After the tornado, however, there was even more labor expected and actually necessary work to be done. So, after partying all night, probably having snuck out of the house, I would get maybe a few hours of sleep then have to work all day with my angry father. He was normally yelling at me all day, rushing me to work faster, and calling me names. "Stupid" was a common one that he liked to use. I remember a number of times after throwing parties there, my dad and I would get to the house and find beer cans all over the place. He would be so mad saying, "Those stupid kids were here partying all night!" oblivious to the fact that I was one of them.

I would laugh on the inside! So I'm the stupid one? I would get in trouble for being drunk all the time! You can't put two and two together? If you don't know what that means, well, the answer is four!

That pretty well sums up my high school experience. There are just two more major stories that I would like to include to finish it off. The first took place at the beginning of my senior year. We had finally moved back into our newly rebuilt house. It was only myself and my younger brother, Joe, still living at home. We were the two youngest kids. My dad was really hard on my little brother, often calling him names and threatening to beat him again. I guess he had gotten in some trouble a couple of times both inside and outside of school. As crazy as my dad was already, the tornado certainly didn't help. It pretty much brought him to complete insanity. It's hard to imagine him getting worse since he was already pretty nuts, but it really pushed him over the edge, probably due to the stress of losing then rebuilding his home.

My point is that he really seemed to have gotten worse and wasn't getting any better. He was being really verbally abusive all the time, enough that my brother actually ran away. We later found out that he went to Florida, not far from where I am right now as I write this on the beach. I love nature and being outside. It's where I find peace as well as writing and other hobbies that I do for myself. I believe he ended up in Daytona Beach, about twenty minutes from New Smyrna Beach, where I live now. It was my brother, Joe, and a couple of friends who brought him down here. I guess he got the idea to come to Florida since that past summer we had been here to visit my sister and her husband, who I stay with now.

I had also run away from home once before, a couple years before Joe did. So, of course, my dad started accusing me from that point on. He blamed me, saying it was my fault he ran away, that Joe got the idea from me. That was the first time ever that I really started standing up to my dad. I went to school the next day, had wrestling practice afterward, then went to my friend, Robert's, house after practice. I refused to go home after how my dad was acting. My mom called and said that he was destroying my stuff. I told her that I still wasn't coming home with that crazy man still there and that I didn't care about my stuff anyway. We eventually found a way to get him out of there which involved calling the police and getting a restraining order against him.

This meant that my parents' relationship was finally over. I was now the only one of six other siblings involved in my parents' divorce, so I testified on my mom's side of course. We found my little brother a week later, and I helped get my mom the house without a man mistreating her there all the time. Now, she is remarried to a man who treats her better, and my dad retired and moved to Colombia. I believe he has now found happiness for the first time in his life, living in another country in peace. He just moved there recently, and the last time we spoke before he left surprisingly ended well.

After the divorce, I actually spoke to my dad frequently. They were normally bad visits and didn't end well. But a lot of that had to do with me still standing up to him and telling him things that I felt he needed to hear. I know I talked a lot about the bad things my father said and did, but he just had problems like everybody else in the world. Only his problems were a little more extreme, and he didn't know how to handle them. I'm fairly certain him being a psychologist didn't help either, hearing other people's problems all the time. Other than his bad side (which was probably about 70 percent of the time), when he was happy, he had one of the best hearts that I have ever seen. He also raised seven great children, so I have to give him credit for that. My siblings are incredible people and some of my best friends in this world.

Now, down to my final high school story; This happened at the end of the school year.

I ended up getting in trouble for some things and going to alternative school which helped me to graduate. But I was done with wrestling, which now meant that the remainder of my time went to partying. I had a best friend that I regularly hung out with.

We were drinking together and drank a lot. I think that we probably drank at least half of gallon of whiskey between the two of us.

My mom had a bad feeling about us being gone. She was panicking and wanting me to come home, so we rushed home for her. But it was dark, raining, and we were drunk, driving down a very windy road. Before I knew it, my friend who was driving had a head-on collision with a telephone pole that totaled the truck. For some reason, in older trucks, they have the option to turn off the passenger airbag so mine was turned off. I wasn't buckled up. There came another concussion! Just what I needed; another head injury. Like I'm not stupid enough!

After being questioned by the police about the alcohol, they rushed me to the hospital. I guess I wasn't needed for treatment too seriously, since they only kept me there an hour. I had a busted eyebrow that required stitches, busted chin, and my two front teeth were broken in half! That's actually what brought me out of my concussion, after refusing pain medicine from the doctors, thinking they were trying to harass me like the cops were. I left the hospital, got back in my mom's vehicle, and pulled down the visor to see my reflection. Looking in the mirror, I realized the fate of my teeth!

I panicked and asked my mom what had happened. She reminded me that I had gotten in a car wreck. The next morning, the whole night came back to me, as well as the pain in my face. (The song "All I Want for Christmas is My Two Front Teeth" came to mind, though I was no longer ten years old!) Fortunately, in spite of our conflicts, my father had compassion on me and helped pay some of the dental bills to have my teeth restored, for which I am very grateful. As I said before, he does have a good heart in spite of his mental illness.

That pretty well covers my high school years. All that is left now is the time from eighteen years old until now (twenty-five), which will conclude my life to where it is now as well as maybe explain why I felt it necessary to write all of these things down. It gives me self-confidence, feeling as though I have accomplished something great. When you've had as many bad things happen in life like I have, you either are kept down from it or choose to do as I do and grow from each and every one of these experiences.

Now that I am back from my break, it is time to finish my story, after having a good meal (that is a way that I reward myself, now that I am sober). My goal today is to finish my writing. I look at it as a way of meditation. I also look at it as my duty as well as a commandment from God. It is something that has been on my mind for five years; to share my story and put it in writing. I know God gives us commandments to help save us from our fallen state, and in writing this book, I look at it as something that may help to fulfill that. It is also something that I enjoy focusing on and enjoy the task given to me from the Lord. I like to think of it as the most important task in the world to accomplish and something that may help the universe as we know it. This is how everyone should view their own lives, for we are all here for a reason right? This is not a bad way of thinking! It is positive thinking that comes from God!

Anything good comes from Him, and of course, anything bad or negative comes from the devil. Any feeling, emotion, or energy that makes me doubt my ability to achieve something does not come from God, but from one of the evil spirits, followers of Satan that want me to fail and feel as miserable as they do. I am too well-trained now to allow that to happen. "Then goeth he, and taketh to him seven other spirits more wicked than himself; and they enter in, and dwell there: and the last state of that man is worse than the first" (Luke 11:29). I have already completed my one task that I was put on this earth to do and conquer.

I know now through spiritual revelation that task was to overcome my addictions, to come back to church, knowing with all my heart that it is true, and is the restored gospel on this earth today.

Illustration by Eliza Robinson

If we do not conquer those spirits that are holding us back, those same spirits will have that same power to possess us in the next life.

> Ye cannot say, when ye are brought to that awful crisis, that I will repent, that I will return to my God. Nay, ye cannot say this; for that same spirit which doth possess your bodies at the time that ye go out of this life, that same spirit will have power to possess your body in that eternal world. (Alma 34:34)

I have already done that by fully overcoming my addictions and am now set to finish my writing today. I feel by doing this, I have already completed my purpose here, which I was called here to do and chosen by God to accomplish. Therefore, His spirit is with me and will stay with me for all eternity. This is because of my faith and what I have been through and overcame. "For many are called, but few are chosen" (Matthew 22:14).

This happened so that I could learn of the power of faith and what can be accomplished with the power of God through His light and eternal progression. All things happen in a timely manner according to God's purpose. There was a war in heaven, and this war led to our existence here on earth and is why we are all here today. This war was necessary in order to create life as we know it.

This was meant to happen so that we could receive physical bodies and be alive today and have a chance to have eternal progression. We are blessed to have the gift of agency, to have a life as we want, full of free choices.

You have agency to choose exactly as you want each day: good, bad, right, wrong, nice, mean, productive, lazy. That's pretty much it; what this world consists of. There are only two forms of energy that make up life as we know it. One leads to happiness, the other leads to sadness. Pretty simple right? That's literally the only purpose of life, to choose which path you care to join. Though we are free to choose however, we cannot choose the consequences of the choices we make. It is as simple as elementary math, adding and subtracting: good/evil, alpha/omega, beginning/end, life/death, male/female, yin/yang. These are a few simple opposites that make up and create everything. It is an eternal creation that has no end, an eternal learning experience. What happens to a star when it dies? It turns into a black hole that sucks/rejuvenates energy from the rest of the universe to create a new galaxy or star to be born again, so that means everyone and everything is made up of "star dust." I guess that is another explanation of God using science as part of the creation. "Matter can neither be created nor destroyed."

Illustration by Mick Hassinger

The stars in the heavens sing a music if only we have ears to hear. (Pythagoras)

Perhaps there is a pattern set up in the heavens for one who desires to see it, and having seen it, to find one in himself. (Plato, Ancient Philosopher)

The celestial bodies are the cause of all that takes place in a sub lunar world. (St. Thomas Aquinas, Catholic saint)

Oh, the wonderful knowledge to be found in the stars. Even the smallest things are written there... If you had but skill to read. (Benjamin Franklin, Founding Father)

We are born at a given moment, in a given place, and like vintage years of wine, we have the qualities of the year and of the season in which we are born. (Carl Gustav Jung, Father of Modern Psychology)

Millionaires don't use astrology, Billionaires do. (JP Morgan, multibillionaire banker)

That is enough schooling in that area, so time to get back to the story of my life: When I was eighteen, I moved to Utah for a few months to work for my brother, Jimmy. I stayed there for the summer. I think I came back home for court. While I did, I decided to stay back in Tennessee. We are known as the "volunteer state." One of my friends invited me to go to a concert in Nashville with him. Before we left, we went to a girl's house so that we could carpool together. Her name was, Tristan. (a.k.a. "Slice Spika," she actually legally changed her name to this at one point and later changed it back. Thinking back, even knowing that information should have made me realize the kind of person that she was.) She was twenty-seven years old but had the mind of child because of a head injury she sustained at eleven years of age. She had been riding a go-cart, and her hair got wrapped in either the chain or the tire, pulling her head back toward the motor where it remained attached for twenty-six minutes to a hot engine. They had to cut her hair and slowly remove her head.

Illustration by Eliza Robinson

She showed me the scars on her head, as well as the square on her butt that they had to remove the skin from to graft on her head. She was literally a butthead! She was also the first love of my life, as well as the first girl that I lived with for a long period of time. By the end of our relationship, we both ended up in a mental hospital. It was my first time going to a place like that. Not hers though. She was quite a few years older than me, and I will give an example of her level of sanity:

My brothers once threw a live rooster into her house as a prank. Technically our house as I was also living there, but everything was hers, as well as the place being in her name. That rooster pretty much became our new pet. She didn't want to get rid of it and not wanting it to die, allowed it to stay there and roam freely as it pleased. This to me shows the state of mind that I was also in at the time for allowing that to happen. There were numerous times that I would wake up in the morning, hearing that rooster crow to sunrise over and over again.

There was also a metal frame that was built over the top of her bed. That was a spot the rooster preferred to stay posted, where it would constantly poop on the bed as well as the rest of the house. We fed the rooster dog food. It stayed there probably a solid month before we finally got rid of it, returning it to where my brothers had gotten it from. By then, it had practically ruined the house and furniture.

Tristan was pretty much a gypsy (as am I after reading its definition): Someone that moves place to place, leaving their belongings behind. That has happened to me a few times as well. She also liked tarot cards and Ouija boards, talking to the dead. Our relationship lasted a full year, until we both ended up in a mental hospital, both of us experiencing psychotic episodes triggered by drug abuse. I ended up staying there an entire month after I had tried to walk on water, carrying a Buddha statue, then walked door to door, knocking on multiple houses looking for mother nature! (By the way, I didn't find her, maybe it was because I wasn't wearing shoes or a shirt.)

Once I was checked into the mental hospital, they forced me to take multiple pills a day. They told me I was schizophrenic and forced me to take a handful of pills three times a day. After being constantly drugged up, I lost my ability to eat, sleep, think clearly, and even talk. I remember hanging out with my brothers and friends, laughing, talking, and having fun. I remember in the back of my mind asking God: *Why me?*

I was terrified that I lost myself and that I would never be the same again, that it was too late to fix the damage that had already happened. I remember thinking back to when I was in high school and that I hadn't always been like this. I used to have a personality. Sometimes, my hands would shake uncontrollably, and I would sometimes even drool. I was struck dumb. I pretty much stayed that way for nearly a year until I slowly recovered back to myself again.

There were a few other times that I had a mental breakdown and went back to a mental hospital. I would normally snap out of that state though in no longer than a couple of months. I realized also that it was pretty much induced by drugs that lead me to that mindset. Unfortunately, it still didn't prevent me from doing what I thought I enjoyed. That pretty much concludes the next chapter of my life which leaves me with one more series of events and also a major part of my life leading me to where I am today! Then, I will conclude this story and explain why I decided to write all of these events down.

Once I finally got out of my cycle of being practically mentally retarded and struck dumb, my mind was beginning to function normally again. I would go to my brother, Adam's, house in Nashville pretty regularly. He had a cool house and would regularly throw big parties.

During one of those parties, I met the friend I mentioned before named Adam (like my brother) Glenn. He was really into MMA (mixed martial arts) fighting, as were a lot of other friends that were there as well, including my brother and his two roommates. That was a big part of their focus at that time, training and preparing for amateur fights.

Adam Glenn and I grappled a lot that night. I was really needing a job, so he told me that he was a contractor and that I could live with him, train MMA with him, and that he had steady work for me. I thought it sounded too good to be true, but it was actually true. He fulfilled his promise and everything that he told me did happen. At the time that we met, he was atheist. Years later, however, he became curious about the church I went to, saying that my brothers and I were some of the best people he had ever met. Therefore, he began to research more and more and changed his ways. He quit his addictions, was baptized, and now is an active member in my church, The Church of Jesus Christ of Latter-Day Saints, also known as Mormons. He joined the church years after this time that we lived together, but during that time, he did fulfill his promise and gave me everything that he said he would. He is a great friend, one of my best friends, and a blessing from God for blessing my life.

I moved in with him that night and now had a nice home, a full-time personal trainer (our boxing coach named Karl Willis whose house we stayed in), and a pretty decent job. Life was looking up for me again. I had what I was looking for and needed in my life. The fact that I was living with MMA fighters was also something I was wanting to get more into and definitely a big plus for me being there as well.

Outside of going to work, the free time that I had in the afternoons was put into training with my boss, sometimes, my other roommate, and my coach, Karl. Sometimes, we would go to the gym, the Clarksville Fight Club, as well. This seemed about the best thing that I could be doing with my free time; exercising and improving my body compared to destroying it with bad substances as well as wasting away time. "Be ye therefore followers of God, as dear children; And walk in love, as Christ also hath loved us, and hath given himself for us an offering and a sacrifice to God for a sweet smelling savor" (Ephesians 5:1–2).

I was currently working for Adam as one of his maintenance workers who helped finalize some of his houses before they were ready to sell. I did anything from hardwood floors, tile, and paint, as well as any miscellaneous cleanup that needed to be done. I probably was doing steady work like this for him at least a month. He later asked me what type of work I wanted to do for him full-time. I told him that I liked to paint. He told me that he already had set painters and that there was a choice of three trades that paid the best as a career and would be in my best interest to choose as a career. The three options that he gave me to choose from were HVAC (heat and air), plumbing, and electrical. These were the three things I suppose charged the contractors the most to do in new home construction, therefore, he wanted to have his own set person to use instead of other companies. This is why he wanted me to be educated in learning one of these three trades to work for him. Out of the three choices he gave me, I picked electrical, which seemed the most interesting to me. As he promised me and said he would do, he found me an electrical job. I now had a good career lined up and now was in the process of becoming an electrician. Life was continuing to get better for me each day. "So that we may boldly say, the Lord is my helper, and I will not fear what man shall do unto me" (Hebrews 13:6).

I soon bought a car and also met a girl that I really liked. I remember spotting her in my brother's house in Nashville at a party he had there. She was the first girl that I laid eyes on when I got there. She was beautiful! I remember spotting the half sleeve tattoo that she had and complimenting her on how I liked it. Afterward, I got on the table there and played some beer pong. My partner and I won many games. We stayed on the table for a while, and I got really drunk. After winning a number of games, we finally lost. My brother had a hot tub at his house, and that was the next thing that I wanted to do after finishing the run of games that we had. Plus, it was pretty much pointless for me to continue drinking, because I was already at a drunk-enough stage for myself. He had a pretty cool house; it was up on a hill right over the city of downtown Nashville.

As I was getting ready to get in the hot tub, I was wanting to find my friend, Myles, to join me as well as a pretty girl to come along as well. I remember asking girl after girl and getting rejected. Then I guess I blacked out. Next thing I remember was coming out of being blacked out and looking up at a girl on my lap kissing me in the hot tub. I saw the half sleeve from the girl I first saw at the beginning of the party. Her name was Joseane! This never happens to me; I was with the girl that I most liked that night and the prettiest girl at the party.

Illustration by Eliza Robinson

The next day, I had a grappling tournament and asked her to come. She came, and as we talked that next day, I found out that she was Brazilian. There were also a lot of Brazilians at that tournament as well. That was the first time that I had ever met anyone from Brazil so looked at it as some kind of sign. I also remember looking at her outside on the school stairs of the tournament we were at. She was so beautiful and kind, so I decided to ask her out that same day. This was something that I never did by the way! She was something special. She had said yes, and I now had a good job, my own place, and a beautiful girlfriend. Life was getting better for me week by week.

I was truly being blessed by God miraculously and did not even realize it at that point of my life. I still had faith and had my regular prayers but that was mostly it as far as anything religious went. "But behold, if ye will awake and arouse your faculties, even to an experiment upon my words, and exercise a particle of faith, yea, even if ye can no more than desire to believe, let this desire work in you, even until ye believe in a manner that ye can give place for a portion of my words" (Alma 32:27).

During these times, I still did drugs and alcohol pretty regularly and was also addicted to nicotine. I introduced her to weed and that was something that we regularly did as a hobby. I was also beginning to do cocaine again. That was a habit I would get hooked on for periods of time and was a continuous problem I had started for myself since early high school. I realized the danger of this addiction having a constant chase and therefore, tried my hardest to get away from this bad habit. This temptation still grasped a hold of me still pretty often. My boxing coach that I lived with liked to smoke it. He would ask me to drive him to the projects sometimes, immediately after I paid him rent. By sometimes, I mean pretty much every time I paid him, and I paid rent every week. Once I paid him and gave him a ride, he let me have some for helping him get what he was wanting to get. I looked at this as getting a free fix on something that I enjoyed doing.

There was more danger in this addiction than I expected. It was a very intense high that lasted for a very short period of time that lead to a very bad constant chase. Before I noticed or even realized for myself, I once again had another bad addiction, and I was now enslaved to this drug. It literally took every bit of anything that I ever made for myself and owned. It took every bit of my money as well as so many different items that I can't even put into writing or remember if I wanted to put it all down. This addiction lasted for over two years. It lasted two years straight as a constant struggle and still became a regular problem again on and off, as well as another two to three years after having it as a regular problem prior to getting better for periods of time. This addiction took three of my cars that I owned. I ended up also stealing my dad's car and selling it as well. "God is our refuge and strength, a very present help in trouble" (Psalm 46:1).

I was now a slave to my addictions as well as to my drug dealers. I would often owe them my next check before even getting paid, and I would also often rent out mine or my girlfriend's car when I had the chance to get a fix after already being broke. A lot of times, she didn't even realize that I loaned out her car. When she found out, she had extreme anger and often threatened to call the cops. There were also many of times I would come home from work with all of my stuff in the yard with her telling me to leave. She still later let me come back nearly every time that I ended up leaving for short periods of time. To make it even worse, I ended up receiving a ten-thousand-dollar settlement from the car wreck that I had in high school during the time of this addiction. That money did not last but a few months. The only two good things that I did with that money was give a decent amount of it to my mom and paid my dad back for the car that I had stolen from him.

The whole experience of being trapped under this addiction was terrible. I would hang out in the projects for hours at a time handing out all of my money and a large percentage of my dope to other addicts to be in their home, so I could get an immediate fix. These dealers often treated me really badly, talking down to me because in their eyes, I was one of the worst people in the world and was just a junkie drug addict. I did not have a problem giving them all of my money and being treated that way. The crazy part was that I was okay with everything that was happening to me and continued to come back. All I cared about was getting my next fix. "Henceforth, I call you not servants; for the servant knoweth not what his Lord doeth: but I have called you friends; for all things that I have heard of my Father I have made known unto you" (John 15:15).

I even, at one point, got beaten practically to death with a pistol. I remember going there and having a gun pointed at me and the guy saying, "Give me your phone and your wallet."

I told him, "No," (actually other words I do not want to repeat in here) and ran up to him and began wrestling him. I thought if I ran I might get shot and did not want to chance that. I felt stronger than him and was taking him to the ground. Next thing I knew, my body went limp, and I was going to the ground. He had hit me in the back of the head with the gun. I was then pistol whipped thirty to fifty times to the face and had my chest stomped in. During this time of being blacked out, I remember being in the worst place I can ever remember being in my life. I was also surrounded by hooded figures. Next thing I knew, I woke up and stood up really fast asking what had happened. I heard in the background someone saying, "Dang, I guess he is a fighter." I'm not really sure how long I was out, but after standing up, I felt my eye swollen shut, as well as my whole face hurting. Someone else said that I should lay back down saying I might have a broken neck. I laid back down and waited for the cops to come where I was then life flighted to Vanderbilt Hospital.

Illustration by Mick Hassinger

I still continued to go back to the projects for a long time even after that incident happening. Most of the reason was because of my stupidity as well as my addiction. A part of it was also the little bit of pride left that I had for myself and showing that I was not scared. I ended up losing everything that I had handed to me because of my addictions. I was given a beautiful girl, a pretty good job, and even a good sum of money for me to start my life, but I messed up because I was not ready for the blessings that I received. Even through all of that craziness, I somehow managed to ask that girl to marry me, and she surprisingly said yes. I am still not really sure why, but our relationship later ended, because I could not quit my worst addiction. Our relationship lasted an entire two years until she was done dealing with a junkie drug addict.

How I managed to keep her that long I am still not really sure, but once she left, it really hit me on how great of a person that I had lost. I then soon realized how terrible my life was going, as well as how big of a problem that I really had. I was in denial for years that there was even anything wrong with me and that I could quit anytime that I wanted to. FIRST STEP TO RECOVERY: ADMIT YOU HAVE A PROBLEM! This is a big step to take and sometimes even harder to realize than you think being blinded by the addiction. After losing the girl of my dreams, I went sober cold turkey again, hoping that it might help me get her back. (There were actually many other times in my life where I became sober for short periods of time.)

Here is the last story that I felt necessary to write down. This happened to me soon after losing my fiancé. I took a trip with my brothers to Gatlinburg in Tennessee. During this time, I was staying sober and committed to God (as I have done many other times in my life) that I would remain drug– and alcohol-free. I was also doing this in hope of showing my ex that I had changed in order to try to win her back. Still, with this being my motivation, I wasn't fully doing it for myself.

During this trip to Gatlinburg, I was staying 100 percent sober, even free from nicotine. But I also had a broken heart, which tends to give me a mental breakdown. I'm not exactly sure of how many other people recognized it, but I knew that I was not my normal self. I was right around the party scene with my brothers but was not participating because of my recent covenant. I took this trip with two of my brothers, Joe and Adam, along with Adam's girlfriend at the time (now wife), Melanie, and her brother, Derek.

As I was currently staying sober, I did not hang out with them the entire time because sometimes, they would go to the bar. There was no reason to go with them, because I was not drinking as well as socially awkward during my mental breakdowns. While they were out drinking, I started talking to some of the other people at our hotel. I noticed that most of them were from other countries. I always found people of other cultures interesting, curious of how they were raised and the background they came from. There was this Asian girl there that I noticed was reading an English book. I decided to talk to her. Her English was broken but we could still communicate. The book she was reading was also in English, so I knew that she could read it pretty well.

Being the person that I am and having a strong testimony of Jesus Christ, I decided to ask her if she knew about my religion. When she said no, I began to tell her about Joseph Smith, who he was, and how he had restored the priesthood on the earth today, which came from Jesus Christ. I will share that same information with any readers now: When Christ was on the earth, He established His church, organizing it with twelve apostles He personally called. He gave them the priesthood authority, power to act in His name and perform the miracles that they did. This priesthood was lost for a period of time after Christ's crucifixion, and as His disciples were slowly killed off one by one. This led to the Dark Ages; a period of time when there was no longer an established gospel that Jesus had brought here.

As time passed, religious freedom was established here in America, paving the way for Christ's true church to be restored to the earth once again. Joseph Smith was instrumental in doing this. He was only a fourteen-year-old boy in the year 1820, when he began to question which church to join. He had a large family with many siblings. They were all baptized into different churches. He wanted to be certain that he was baptized in the right church.

One day, as he was reading the Bible, he came across the scripture James 1:5, "If any of ye lack wisdom, let him ask of God."

This scripture really spoke to Joseph. He went into the woods, knelt down, and prayed to God. As he prayed, he was overpowered by what he described to be an evil spirit, Satan who was determined to prevent him from doing this.

> But, exerting all my powers to call upon
> God to deliver me out of the power of this enemy
> which had seized upon me, and at the very
> moment, when I was ready to sink into despair

and abandon myself to destruction—not to an imaginary ruin, but to the power of some actual being from the unseen world, who had such marvelous power as I had never before felt in any being—just at this moment of great alarm, I saw a pillar of light exactly over my head, above the brightness of the sun, which descended gradually until it fell upon me.

It no sooner appeared than I found myself delivered from the enemy which held me bound. When the light rested upon me, I saw two personages, whose brightness and glory defy all description, standing above me in the air. One of them spoke unto me, calling me by name and said, pointing to the other—this is My Beloved Son. Hear Him! (Joseph Smith History 1:16–17).

When our heavenly Father and His Son, Jesus, Christ appeared unto Joseph Smith, they told him that none of the churches had the fullness of the gospel. "They draw near to me with their lips, but their hearts are far from me" (Joseph Smith History 1:19).

Other heavenly messengers came to Joseph Smith over time, as he was called to be a prophet in these latter-days. One of them was an angel, Moroni, who revealed to him an ancient record of scripture inscribed on plates of gold, buried in the earth until he was led to them. Through the power of God, he was able to translate them into what is known today as *The Book of Mormon: Another Testament of Jesus Christ.* It's words contain records of ancient inhabitants of the Americas, some who may have been the Mayans, Aztecs, ancestors of the American Indians before white men, found this land hundreds of years later. It also talks about how Jerusalem was being destroyed, even during the Tower of Babel, and how a prophet Lehi and his family were commanded to travel the oceans to start a new life in a land they called the "promised land." This began the history of *The Book of Mormon*, which also talks about how Christ visited this land following His resurrection.

Through Joseph Smith, these lost records were restored, as well as the priesthood power and Christ's true church, which is why it is now called The Church of Jesus Christ of Latter-Day Saints. It is His same church, in these latter days. Joseph Smith's testimony was so devout, he even died as a martyr for what he knew to be true. I do not think that someone would put this much effort into creating a false church. This also goes to show over the records of time, how evil people become with jealousy when they see light from God. History constantly repeats itself.

I did not go into this much detail with the girl from China that I met, but I felt that now seemed like an appropriate time to write this down. I did explain most of this doctrine to her just in less detail and in fewer words. After I was done, I asked her if she wanted a Bible and she said, "Yes!" Therefore, I gave her a *King James Bible* that I had, and she took it. She gave me a book written in Chinese and told me that I would learn that book as well. I did not know how that seemed possible since the only thing that seemed readable on it was the twelve zodiacs drawn on it in a circle on the front cover. I believe that this event happened the night before we left from our vacation.

The next day, I saw all of the foreign people that were there outside the next morning. They varied from all parts of the world as far as the different locations and countries that they came from. Later, as they were all sitting there, I saw this creepy old man coming up to them looking angry and asking where the rest of their group went; it seemed that a large percent of them were gone. He was asking but seemed to already know as he said, "They left, right?"

As he was asking that, he was also rubbing his foot against the girl I had been talking to and asked, "Who wants a new phone?" That left me a weird vibe with this old man and what his intentions were and what he was wanting with these young foreign adults (both male and female). There was more I wanted to do about the situation I saw there but did not know what to do and it was about the time we were leaving anyways. I left, always remembering that vacation, all the foreign people from all over the world I had seen there, and most of all, the girl from Asia that I met, the conversations that we had, and the books that we exchanged before I left.

I went back to doing my electrical job. I think that I was also looking for a new place to live since I was living in my ex's house and we had broken up. I also did not have a car, so I was cycling everywhere that I went. I sold my car being broke and wanting to get some fast money. I believe I drove that car into a scrap yard. Fastest way I knew to get guaranteed cash. Even without having a home or a car, I was still able to maintain a job. That had only lasted a couple of more weeks because even though I was staying sober, I was also going through another mental breakdown having the hardest breakup of my life. That being from the woman I had planned to marry and spend the rest of my life with. Even with staying sober and showing up to work every day, that was not enough, and I had lost my job. My work performance went down being in the mental state that I was in, and I was also weirding out my work employees doing things out of the ordinary at work that a normal worker should not be doing.

I am not even sure if they recognized the mindset that I was in but had to see me as not being my normal self. See, every time that I have a mental breakdown, my mind practically becomes possessed. I start hearing voices that I listen to that tell my body and mind to do unusual things. A lot of times, it has to do with thinking that if I grab certain things that I find and place them in a particular order that something magical would happen in doing so. I would constantly do this every day for months at a time. I guess I wasn't doing it right because nothing ever happened, but my mind thought otherwise, and I continued to try and do this.

My work could only handle so much of these actions and decided to let me go. I remember this happening the weekend of the fourth of July. I remember asking my boss why I had not gotten paid for the holiday when everyone else did. That was when he told me he had to let me go. This was early in the work day, and I decided there was no point in me finishing the day. My crew leader even had the nerve to ask me if I was going to finish the day. I told him no and walked off the job with my tools. This had also happened about a week before my years paid week off. That would have been the first time that a company ever gave me a paid week off, but I did not quite make the cut on that one. I was now homeless, carless, and from that point on, officially jobless!

All of these things happened to me being blinded by my addictions and from the actions that I made to those that surrounded me in my life, I slowly pushed them away one by one. I now had lost my fiancé, most of my close friends, and pretty much my family as well. Nobody could trust me for what I had turned into and who I became. I remember one time asking my mom if I could stay there needing somewhere to sleep. She and her husband, Mike (my stepdad), said, "No way!" They did bring me some canned food though and gave me a ride to the salvation army where I could sleep at the homeless shelter.

Since I no longer had a job, I would regularly cycle through the town, listening to music, to try and clear my mind. One day, I came across these people in a parking lot handing out tie-dyed T-shirts. This immediately attracted my attention being a hippie at heart. This was also near where I used to work, therefore, a place I cycled in my regular daily route. Well I went up to these people which were mostly girls, asked the occasion in why they were doing this, and if I could have a shirt.

They gave me a shirt and explained to me how this was part of them promoting school for the next summer semester of massage therapy about to start. They directed me in what to do to be part of this summer course and how to sign up.

They said if I took this test and passed, as well as qualified for the school loans, then I would get my school paid for upfront by the government as well as get some money upfront for myself to help while I was in school. I took them up on this offer and decided to try to find out if this was all true. To my surprise, it all was, and I actually passed the test to be qualified for the school. I was shocked that I even passed this test being years that I had even taken a test, as well as years of partying and increased damage to my brain. All of this worked out, and I received everything as promised. I was also able to find a place to stay with some old family church friends. Things were starting to look better again in my life. I cycled back-and-forth to school and was on my way to learning a new profession.

Massage therapy taught me the anatomy of the body. I learned how the body was made up as well as all of the bones and muscles. It was a lot of information crammed into a small period of time. After some of these hard classes like anatomy and physiology, kinesiology, and somatic patterning (which was practically psychology) which made up the first half of the day; the second half of the day we would do yoga, meditate, and practice massages on one another. We would take turns learning different trades and skills on how to do different techniques and routines to use. We also learned proper body mechanics to use to prevent injury when giving massages for long periods of time. Even working hard long summer construction jobs, this school seemed to drain me even more than that did by being mentally hard and challenging the brain in different ways. In school, my teachers would sometimes joke and call our school advanced preschool with us breaking up the hard classes with hands on training and some of the fun things that we did to be trained in that way.

Illustration by Eliza Robinson

While cycling home from school one day, I got hit by a car. I was pretty upset about this incident, I had just tuned up my bike and put a decent amount of money into it. This totaled my bicycle.

I did not break any bones; luckily my face broke my fall and the only injury that I had was my tooth breaking through my lip, leaving some stitches needed in the face and my right shoulder and arm getting some road rash. An officer was wanting to get my information and hear my side of the story. I did not want to talk to him. I was hurting and upset about the whole ordeal. He made me give him my ID and told me he would later be visiting me at the hospital. He later showed up there and told me that I had been charged for a yielding violation. I told him that it was not my fault and that they did not have a turn signal, therefore, I ran through the light with traffic thinking they were going straight. He told me I had to go to court and that I could take that up with the judge.

With that being the case, I asked my old soccer coach, Rod Martin, who was a lawyer if he would represent me for court. He told me that he would represent me no charge being a longtime family friend. We scheduled a date to meet up where we could talk about this in person. I was on a different bike that I also had and was cycling downtown so that I could meet him. The Holy Ghost had warned me to be careful looking at this truck that was to my right, ready to pull out. I ignored that feeling (like I had many of times in my past and later regretted it) and assumed that surely, this truck had seen me coming down the hill. Well, I guess that it didn't, and I was once again hit by another vehicle. I was laying there in the road and he stopped for a minute, but once he saw me get up and yell at him in anger, he quickly took off, realizing I was okay and not wanting to deal with the charge. I found this kind of ironic in the timing of when I was hit again. Thankfully, I was not hurt as bad, I did not need to go to the hospital or need stitches this time, and my bike was still rideable. After picking up my stuff and fixing my bike I continued on to go see my lawyer and told him once again what had happened. He was kind of bothered about what I had told him and told me that I needed to be more careful.

My charge was dropped in court, and I continued on with my schooling. This was a story I felt compelled to write down, showing, in my opinion, how unfair I think the court system can be sometimes, also the irony of me getting hit by another vehicle while going to talk to my lawyer about the prior incident recently before that.

Here are some more information that I learned while going to college: first of all, the main book that we used which was our massage therapy book was written by Patricia J. Benjamin. Therefore, they referred to this book in school as the "Benjamin Bible." I also learned that it had an Asian background and has been practiced for thousands of years now. This was something taught and commonly done there to naturally heal the body by manipulating the muscle tissues with massage oils. I also took another class that really stood out to me called Energy and was probably my favorite class in school. In this class, we learned how everything is made up of energy, also how all people carry an aura that pushes out at a radius of six feet. This is something unseen by the average eye, but it is said that some people are able to see other people's auras. It was also said that sometimes people don't connect well right when they first meet, perhaps because of their auras putting off different energies that don't mix the same beings opposites and giving each other bad vibes. Lastly, I also learned about the seven chakras that go through the body.

These are listed in order head to toe:

1. crown chakra
2. third eye chakra
3. throat chakra
4. heart chakra
5. solar plexus chakra
6. sacral chakra
7. root chakra

I did not complete school. I went back to my addictions about half way through the program, dropped out two thirds of the way done, then soon went to jail. This was a cycle that I was used to doing throughout my life. Kind of like a roller coaster of doing good and bad having its random ups and downs, as well as those sudden loop de loops unexpected. With all this being said and through these last few stories I mentioned, this goes back to the Chinese girl that I met in Gatlinburg. I remember her giving me that book written in Chinese with the zodiac symbols on it. I felt that I learned her book and pray that she may have read and learned that Bible that I gave her. The Lord works in mysterious ways.

The Mormon church also teaches how we were all with God before we came to the Earth in what we call our "preexistence." That we were and still are God's spirit children, how we saw that He had a body and that there was a plan made so that we could all receive and obtain mortal bodies as well. There were actually two plans made. One plan came from Jesus Christ, and through His plan, we would all have the choice between good and evil to make our own decisions and decide the path that we would each take. He said that He would atone for our sins that even messing up we would be forgiven giving God all the glory. The other plan was from Lucifer who wanted to force everyone to do good, not giving us free agency, and he wanted recognition and all of the glory to himself. This led to a big war in heaven that led to a whole third of God's spirit children following Lucifer or now "the Devil" getting kicked out of heaven and losing their opportunity to come to Earth, receive a mortal body, and getting the chance to experience life here. On Earth we are tested to see the next stage of eternity that we are worthy of receiving and where we will feel most comfortable. The past was yesterday, the present is today, and our future is tomorrow. "Jesus Christ is the same yesterday, and today, and forever" (Hebrews 13:8).

As far as I am concerned, what others may fail to realize is that this war in heaven was meant to happen! This was part of God's plan in giving us mortals the decision to choose between right and wrong. We would not have these feelings or emotions without the devil and spirits that chose to follow him. This is also what led to the existence of life for many of us, without this war in heaven we may not have ever had this life, and this WAR is still going on. Waiting on us to make decisions and actions on how we are going to help our ETERNAL FAMILY! It is also easier to blame all of our problems on one spirit and him being the problem than us taking credit for our own actions. "I search but never find, hurt but never cry, I work and forever try, but I'm cursed, so never mind" (Tunches).

What do I know though, I am just a laborer enslaved to the dollar bill. I learned in college that according to the zodiacs and the Chinese calendar, I am the cross between a metal goat and a lion. No, wait I am lying, through psychedelic trips I know that I am spiritually a dragon. As far as I can tell, life is all about the Benjamin's but this is just a metaphor.

> Now if this is boasting, even so will I boast; for this is my life and my light, my joy and my salvation, and my redemption from everlasting wo. Yea, blessed is the name of my God, who has been mindful of this people, who are a branch of the tree of Israel, and has been lost from its body in a strange land; yea, I say, blessed be the name of my God, who has been mindful of us, wanderers in a strange land. (Alma 26:36)

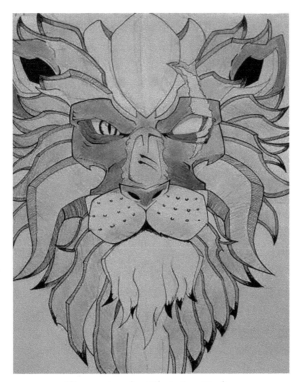

Illustration by Christian Probst

Well, just as I said before, I did not finish my school and ended up in jail soon after dropping out. Part of me giving up on myself was realizing even after going to school and getting sober my ex would not take me back. I went back to my old ways thinking that it would fix or help relieve the pain that I had inside. "You will seek me and find me, when you search for me with all your heart. I will be found by you, says the Lord" (Jeremiah 29:13 and 14). That was only a trick that continued to keep me down. It took me two more years of trial and error until I realized that I really needed help and checked myself into a six-month inpatient rehab to get some help. Even then, I did not fully do it for myself, I also did it to help me with my legal troubles.

I did make some progress, but by the end of rehab, I was still using nicotine, regularly drinking alcohol, and using other supplements on occasion. I received some blessings still for trying to turn my life around that year and focusing some of my attention more toward the Lord than in the past. I had gotten out of the court system and was done with my legal troubles.

I also scored a really good job through my brother, Adam, working on cell phone towers with the company he worked for. "The Lord is righteous in all His ways, and holy in all His works. The Lord is nigh unto all them that call upon Him, to all that call upon Him in truth. He will fulfill the desire of them that fear Him: He also will hear their cry and will save them" (Psalm 145:17–19).

After receiving this job, I soon started messing with a bad addiction that I had done in the past. I was not functioning properly at work and once again lost another blessing that I had just received from God. There are so many other events and stories that I could write down, but it does not matter. I need to get to my conclusion of my story and where I am at now. I think that I made my point multiple times of all the highs and lows that I regularly had for myself. Thinking all is lost, that I was hopeless, and had no chances left. That there was nothing else that I could do. I even had suicidal thoughts. I was not even capable of doing that, being the religious person that I am, and too worried about what would happen to my soul.

I am a living example of somebody that has hit rock bottom in multiple ways and on multiple occasions. I am also somebody that learns by falling. "Fear is how I fall, confusing what is real" -Linkin Park. I also pay attention to movies and how does Buzz Lightyear say it? "That's falling with style!" I now have a PhD in sobriety! I had a vision once of also a preborn psychologist giving my father the schooling before I was born. I have had multiple head injuries but can function just as well as the average person. I choose to grow from every experience that I go through in a positive way, finding a positive out of every negative thing that has ever happened to me. This is the way that I choose to think!

My Testimony

I am now barely over two months sober, but in these past two months, I have accomplished so much. I believe that I will never fall again, and if I do, I will never fall down the same path as before. I have my sister, Mary Kay, and her husband (my brother-in-law), Tim, to thank for bringing me in and helping me to where I am today. I also have my church to thank and the gospel that it teaches as well as the truth and light that it brings. I have seen so many of the active members here having natural happiness; true happiness that only comes from one light.

I had my mind set on serving a two-year mission for this church, The Church of Jesus Christ of Latter-Day Saints. I allowed myself to get sober with this goal in mind. I later found out last night that because of my past, I was not allowed to serve this two-year mission that I had in mind. I just gained back two years of my life that I thought that I had lost. I was hoping to serve God for two years, learn His gospel like the back of my hand, and bring many to His restored church that is on this earth today. I found out that because of my past, I was not allowed to go on this type of mission. I, once again, hit rock bottom. I thought that all was lost. The old me would have gone back to my addictions and would have given up on all that I had accomplished. The new me says otherwise!

I was so down this morning it was ridiculous! I did not even want to get out of bed or go to work. What do I do when I fall down? I get back up! The spirit told me to get out of bed and finish my writing, so this is what I did. I wrote all day and all night until I finished what is almost done. I even took a six-hour break and helped Kimberly (the investigator of the church I wrote about previously) move into her new home. I could have gone to sleep—the old me would have, but the new me says finish! Accomplish what I have already started and am so close to finishing! Why give up now? My favorite scripture verse is: "Let your light so shine before men, that they may see your good works, and glorify your Father which is in heaven" (Matthew 5:16).

I know that with all of my heart that God's records are real! I know that God is real! That every creation is because of Him, and that is why we are all here: to learn and grow! I know that there are many religions and that they each have their own purpose.

I know that with all of my heart that Jesus is the Christ that atoned for our sins.

> For it is expedient that an atonement should be made; for according to the great plan of the Eternal God, there must be an atonement made, or else all mankind must unavoidably perish; yea, all are hardened; yea all are fallen and are lost and must perish except it be through the atonement which is expedient should be made. (Alma 34:9)

I know that because of that, we are all forgiven for all of our sins. I know that through Jesus and by Him, that all things are possible! Faith is like a little seed, if you plant it, it grows!

Illustration by Mick Hassinger

Now, we will compare the word unto a seed. Now, if ye give place, that a seed may be planted in your heart, behold, if it be a true seed, or a good seed, if ye do not cast it out by your unbelief, that ye will resist the Spirit of the Lord, behold it will begin to swell within your breasts; and when you feel these swelling motions, ye will begin to say within yourselves—It must needs be that this is a good seed, or that the word is good, for it beginneth to enlarge my soul; yea, it beginneth to enlighten my understanding, yea, it beginneth to be delicious to me.

Now behold, would not this increase your faith? I say unto you, Yea; nevertheless, it hath not grown up to a perfect knowledge. But behold, as the seed swelleth, and sprouteth, and beginneth to grow. And now, behold, will not this strengthen your faith? Yea, it will strengthen your faith: for ye will say I know that this is a good seed; for behold it sprouteth and beginneth to grow. And now, behold, are ye sure that this is a good seed? I say unto you, Yea; for every seed bringethforth unto its own likeness. Therefore, if a seed groweth it is good, but if it groweth not, behold it is not good, therefore, it is cast away. And now, behold, because ye have tried the experiment, and planted the seed, and it swelleth and sprouteth, and beginneth to grow, ye must needs know that the seed is good. And now, behold, is your knowledge perfect? Yea, your knowledge is perfect in that thing, and your faith is dormant; and this because you know, for ye know that the word hath swelled your souls, and ye also know that it hath sprouted up, that your understanding doth begin to expand. Then, is not this real? I say unto you, Yea, because it is light; and whatsoever is light, is good, because it is discernible, therefore, ye must know that it is good; and now behold, after ye have tasted this light is your knowledge perfect?

Behold I say unto you, Nay; neither must ye lay aside your faith, for ye have only exercised your faith to plant the seed that ye might try the experiment to know if the seed was good. And behold, as the tree beginneth to grow, ye will say: Let us nourish it with great care, that it may get root, that it may grow up, and bring forth fruit unto us. And now, behold, if ye nourish it with much care it will get root, and grow up, and bring forth fruit. But if ye neglect the tree, and take no thought for its nourishment, behold, it will not get any root; and when the heat of the sun cometh and scorcheth it, because it hath no root it withers away, and ye pluck it up and cast it out.

Now, this is not because the seed was not good, neither is it because the fruit thereof would not be desirable; but it is because your ground is barren, and ye will not nourish the tree, therefore, ye cannot have the fruit thereof. And thus, if ye will not nourish the word, looking forward with an eye of faith to the fruit thereof, ye can never pluck of the fruit of the tree of life. But if ye will nourish the word, yea, nourish the tree as it beginneth to grow, by your faith with great diligence and with patience, looking forward to the fruit thereof, it shall take root; and behold, it shall be a tree springing up unto everlasting life. And because of your diligence and your faith and your patience with the word in nourishing it, that it may take root in you, behold, by and by ye shall pluck the fruit thereof, which is most precious, which is sweet above all that is sweet, and which is white above all that is white, yea, and pure above all that is pure; and ye shall feast upon this fruit even until ye are filled, that ye hunger not, neither shall ye thirst. Then, my brethren, ye shall reap the rewards of your faith, and your diligence, and patience, and long-suffering, waiting for the tree to bring forth fruit unto you. (Alma 32:28–43)

Illustration by Dorthy Ledbetter

I know that Joseph Smith is a true prophet that restored the priesthood on this earth today. I know he did this by FAITH and even died for what he believed in, just like every other great individual that lived here and died for what they believe in.

> Yea, even that ye would have so much faith as even to plant the word in your hearts, that ye may try the experiment of its goodness. And we have beheld that the great question which is in your minds is whether the word be in the Son of God, or whether there shall be no Christ. And ye also beheld that my brother has proved unto you, in many instances, that the word is in Christ unto salvation. (Alma 34:4–6)

I know that every book that was ever written comes from God, for He is everything! I know the *Book of Mormon* to be the newest and most true recent record on this Earth today. I know that it was translated by Joseph Smith through God directly! I know that these records were written on golden plates and after being translated, were given to the angel Moroni to have these records physically kept and restored in heaven! They were only translated by one person and were not edited and changed by multiple writers over the years. I know this to be a true book that I cannot wait to finish reading. I know this with all of my heart and have never been more positive of something in my entire life.

I know that anybody that takes Moroni's challenge will know this as well. His challenge is that if you read the Book of Mormon start to finish with a sincere heart, you will know it to be true and the spirit or Holy Ghost will tell you these things.

> And when ye shall receive these things, I would exhort you that ye would ask God, the Eternal Father, in the name of Christ, if these things are not true; and if ye shall ask with a sincere heart, with real intent, having faith in Christ, He will manifest the truth of it unto you, by the power of the Holy Ghost. (Moroni 10:4)

Moroni was named after Captain Moroni and here are some great words written about him:

> And Moroni was a strong and a mighty man; he was a man of a perfect understanding; yea, a man that did not delight in bloodshed; a man whose soul did joy in the liberty and the freedom of his country, and his brethren from bondage and slavery; Yea, a man whose heart did swell with thanksgiving to his God, for the many privileges and blessings which he bestowed upon his people; a man who did labor exceedingly for the welfare and safety of his people. Yea, and he was a man who was firm in the faith of Christ, and he

had sworn with an oath to defend his people, his rights, and his country, and his religion, even to the loss of his blood. Yea, verily, verily I say unto you, if all men had been, and were, and ever would be, like unto Moroni, behold, the very powers of hell would have been shaken forever; yea, the devil would never have power over the hearts of the children of men. (Alma 11:13 and 17)

I know that with God, everything is possible. I know to get where I am today, I had to rewire my brain. Thankfully, I am an electrician and know how to do this. I know that my writing skills have gone down from such a long day of writing haha. I know that I am at peace with myself for finishing what I felt was my job to do. I know that the last chapter of the *Book of Mormon* directly speaks of me. It says that my blessing speaks of the word of wisdom (the law of health preventing things harmful for the body and not to consume in the body).

I know that we are all God's children, therefore, in some way, shape, or form, we helped create the universe. I know that everybody has some sort of purpose here, and their job is to find and accomplish it. I know that I was directed by God to write my life down. I know that because of that I will bless many lives. I know that my sister and brother-in-law will help me to do this because it is in the name of God. I know that this life is about trial and error and that is the beauty of life and Christ's atonement. You have as many chances as you need necessary to get things right and that all things are possible in the name of Jesus Christ. I know that everybody here is equal and that we each chose the lives we have for a greater purpose, knowing that each purpose is just as important as the next!

I know that all of us have something that we each struggle with. I know we can overcome whatever that problem is if we choose to do so. I know that because of the fall of Adam, we are here today. I know that Eve recognized the importance of this life and how it would make us more God—like experiencing it. This is why she partook of the fruit of knowledge (of good and evil) from Lucifer and why she is the mother of all living.

I know that everybody has some sort of fear to overcome, and if we give religion a chance to work like it is supposed to, we can come out of our fallen state if we all work together as a family that we all are, just confused as the next! "But I tell you of a truth, there be some standing here, which shall not taste of death, till they see the kingdom of God" (Luke 9:27).

I know that I am a literal thinker that tries to think logically. I wish I could tell you what that means, but I have no idea what that means! May the force be with you! Or how my school has taught me to close Namaste Day! I say these things so humbly in the name of Jesus Christ, Amen! "Champions are born to be made... Everybody is one!"

And now, behold, I say unto you, my brethren, you that belong to this church, have you sufficiently retained in remembrance the captivity of your fathers? Yea, and have you sufficiently retained in remembrance his mercy and long-suffering towards them? And moreover, have ye sufficiently retained in remembrance that he has delivered their souls from hell? Behold, he changed their hearts; yea, he awakened them out of a deep sleep, and they awoke unto God. Behold, they were in the midst of darkness; nevertheless, their souls were illuminated by the light of the everlasting word; yea, they were encircled about by the bands of death, and the chains of hell, and an everlasting destruction did await them.

And now I ask of you, my brethren, were they destroyed? Behold, I say unto you, Nay, they were not. And again, I ask, were the bands of death broken, and the chains of hell which encircled them about, were they loosened? I say unto you, yea, they were loosed, and their souls did expand, and they did sing redeeming love. And I say unto you that they are saved. And now I ask of you on what conditions are they saved? Yea, what grounds have they to hope for salvation? What is the cause of their being loosed from the bands of death, yea, and also the chains of hell?

Behold, I can tell you—did not my father Alma believe in the words which were delivered by the mouth of Abinadi? And was he not a holy prophet? Did he not speak the words of God, and my father Alma believe them? And according to his faith there was a mighty change wrought in his heart. Behold, I say unto you that this is all true. And behold, he preached the word unto your fathers, and a mighty change was also wrought in their hearts, and they humbled themselves and put their trust in the true and living God. And behold, they were faithful until the end; therefore, they were saved. And now behold, I ask of you, my brethren of the church, have ye spiritually been born of God? Have ye received his image in your countenances? Have ye experienced this mighty change in your hearts? Do ye exercise faith in the redemption of him who created you? Do you look forward with an eye of faith, and view this mortal body raised in immortality, and this corruption raised in incorruption, to stand before God to be judged according to the deeds which have been done in the mortal body?

I say unto you, can you imagine to yourselves that ye hear the voice of the Lord, saying unto you, in that day: Come unto me ye blessed, for behold, your works have been the works of righteousness upon the face of the earth? Or do ye imagine to yourselves that ye can lie unto the Lord in that day, and say—Lord, our works have been righteous works upon the face of the earth—and that he will save you? Or otherwise, can ye imagine yourselves brought before the tribunal of God with your souls filled with guilt and remorse, having a remembrance of all your guilt, yea, a perfect remembrance of all your wickedness, yea, a remembrance that ye have set at defiance the commandments of God? I say unto you, can ye look up to God at that day with a pure heart and clean hands? I say unto you, can you look up, having the image of God engraven upon your countenances? I say unto you, can ye think of being saved when you have yielded yourselves to become subjects to the devil?

I say unto you, ye will know at that day that ye cannot be saved; for there can no man be saved except his garments are washed white; yea, his garments must be purified until they are cleansed from all stain, through the blood of him of whom it has been spoken by our fathers, who should come to redeem his people from their sins. And now I ask of you, my brethren, how will any of you feel, if ye shall stand before the bar of God, having your garments stained with blood and all manner of filthiness? Behold, what will these things testify against you? Behold will they not testify that ye are murderers, yea, and also that ye are guilty of all manner of wickedness? Behold, my brethren, do ye suppose that such one can have a place to sit down in the kingdom of God, with Abraham, with Isaac, and with Jacob, and also all the holy prophets, whose garments are cleansed and are spotless, pure and white? I say unto you, Nay; except ye make our Creator a liar from the beginning or suppose that he is a liar from the beginning, ye cannot suppose that such can have place in the kingdom of heaven; but they shall be cast out for they are the children of the kingdom of the devil.

And now behold, I say unto you, my brethren, if ye have experienced a change of heart, and if ye have felt to sing the song of redeeming love, I would ask, can ye feel so now? Have ye walked, keeping yourselves blameless before God? Could ye say, if ye were called to die at this time, within yourselves, that ye have been sufficiently humble? That your garments have been cleansed and made white through the blood of Christ, who will come to redeem his people from their sins? Behold, are ye stripped of pride? I say unto you, if ye are not ye are not prepared to meet God. Behold, ye must prepare quickly; for the kingdom of heaven is soon at hand, and such an one hath not eternal life. Behold, I say, is there one among you who is not stripped of envy? I say unto you that such an one is not prepared; and I would that he should prepare quickly, for the hour is close at hand, and he knoweth not when the time shall come; for such an one is not found guiltless.

And again, I say unto you, is there one among you that doth make a mock of his brother, or that heapeth upon him persecutions? Wo unto such an one, for he is not prepared, and the time is at hand that he must repent or he cannot be saved! Yea, even wo unto all ye workers of iniquity; repent, repent, for the Lord God hath spoken it! Behold, he sendeth an invitation unto all men, for the arms of mercy are extended towards them, and he saith: Repent, and I will receive you. Yea, he saith: Come unto me and ye shall partake of the fruit of the tree of life; yea, ye shall eat and drink of the bread and the waters of life freely; Yea, come unto me and bring forth works of righteousness, and ye shall not be hewn down and cast into the fire—for behold, the time is at hand that whosoever bringeth forth not good fruit, or whosoever doeth not the works of righteousness, the same have cause to wail and mourn. O ye workers of iniquity; ye that are puffed up in the vain things of the world, ye that have professed to have known the ways of righteousness nevertheless have gone astray, as sheep having no shepherd, notwithstanding a shepherd hath called after you and is still calling after you, but ye will not hearken unto his voice! Behold, I say unto you, that the good shepherd doth call you; yea, and in his own name he doth call you, which is the name of Christ; and if ye will not hearken unto the voice of the good shepherd, to the name by which ye are called, behold, ye are not the sheep of the good shepherd. And now if ye are not the sheep of the good shepherd, of what fold are ye? Behold, I say unto you, that the devil is your shepherd, and ye are of his fold; and now, who can deny this? Behold, I say unto you, whosoever denieth this is a liar and a child of the devil. For I say unto you that whatsoever is good cometh from God, and whatsoever is evil cometh from the devil.

Therefore, if a man bringeth forth good works he hearkeneth unto the voice of the good shepherd, and he doth follow him; but whosoever bringeth forth evil works, the same becometh a child of the devil, for he hearkeneth unto his voice, and doth follow him. And whosoever doeth this must receive his wages of him; therefore, for his wages he receiveth death, as to things pertaining unto righteousness, being dead unto all good works. And now, my brethren, I would that ye should hear me, for I speak in the energy of my soul; for behold, I have spoken unto you plainly that ye cannot err or have spoken according to the commandments of God. For I am called to speak after this manner, according to the holy order of God, which is in Christ Jesus; yea, I am commanded to stand and testify unto this people the things which have been spoken by our fathers concerning the things which are to come. And this is not all. Do ye not suppose that I know of these things myself? Behold, I testify unto you that I do know that these things whereof I have spoken are true. And how do ye suppose that I know of their surety? Behold, I say unto you they are made known unto me by the Holy Spirit of God. Behold, I have fasted and prayed many days that I might know these things of myself. And now I do know of myself that they are true; for the Lord God hath made them manifest unto me by his Holy Spirit; and this is the spirit of revelation which is in me.

And moreover, I say unto you that it has thus been revealed unto me, that the words which have been spoken by our fathers are true, even so according to the spirit of prophecy which is in me, which is also by the manifestation of the Spirit of God. I say unto you, that I know of myself that whatsoever I shall say unto you, concerning that which is to come, is true; and I say unto you, that I know that Jesus Christ shall come, yea, the Son, the Only Begotten of the Father, full of grace, and mercy, and truth. And behold, it is he that cometh to take away the sins of the world, yea, the sins of every man who steadfastly believeth on his name. And now,

I say unto you that this is the order after which I am called, yea, to preach unto my beloved brethren, yea, and every one that dwelleth in the land; yea, to preach unto all, both old and young, both bond and free; yea, I say unto you the aged, and also the middle aged, and the rising generation; yea, to cry unto them that they must repent and be born again. Yea, thus saith the Spirit: Repent, all ye ends of the earth, for the kingdom of heaven is soon at hand; yea, the Son of God cometh in his glory, in his might, majesty, power, and dominion. Yea, my beloved brethren, I say unto you, that the Spirit saith: Behold the glory of the King of all the earth; and also, the King of heaven shall very soon shine forth among all the children of men. And also, the Spirit saith unto me, yea, crieth unto me with a mighty voice, saying: Go forth and say unto this people—Repent, for except ye repent ye can in nowise inherit the kingdom of heaven. And again, I say unto you, the Spirit saith: Behold, the ax is laid at the root of the tree; therefore, every tree that bringeth not forth good fruit shall be hewn down and cast into the fire, yea, a fire which cannot be consumed, even an unquenchable fire.

Behold, and remember, the Holy One hath spoken it. And now my beloved brethren, I say unto you, can ye withstand these sayings; yea, can ye lay aside these things, and trample the Holy One under your feet; yea, can ye be puffed up in the pride of your hearts; yea, will ye still persist in the wearing of costly apparel and setting your hearts upon the vain things of the world, upon your riches? Yea, will ye persist in supposing that ye are better one than another; yea, will ye persist in the persecution of your brethren, who humble themselves and do walk after the holy order of God, wherewith they have been brought into this church, having been sanctified by the Holy Spirit, and finally, all ye that will persist in your wickedness, I say unto you that these are they who shall be hewn down and cast into the fire except they speedily repent.

And now I say unto you, all you that are desirous to follow the voice of the good shepherd, come ye out from the wicked, and be ye separate, and touch not their unclean things; and behold, their names shall be blotted out, that the names of the wicked shall not be numbered among the names of the righteous, that the word of God may be fulfilled, which saith: The names of the wicked shall not be mingled with the names of my people; for the names of the righteous shall be written in the book of life, and unto them will I grant an inheritance at my right hand.

And now, my brethren, what have ye to say against this? I say unto you, if ye speak against it, it matters not, for the word of God must be fulfilled. For what shepherd is there among you having many sheep doth not watch over them, that the wolves enter not and devour his flock? And behold, if a wolf enters his flock, doth he not drive him out? Yea, and at the last, if he can, he will destroy him. And now I say unto you that the good shepherd doth call after you; and if you will hearken unto his voice he will bring you into his fold, and ye are his sheep; and he commandeth you that ye suffer no ravenous wolf to enter among you, that ye may not be destroyed. And now I, Alma, do command you in the language of him who hath commanded me, that ye observe to do the words which I have spoken unto you. I speak by way of command unto you that belong to the church; and unto those who do not belong to the church I speak by way of invitation, saying: Come and be baptized unto repentance, that ye also may be partakers of the fruit of the tree of life. (Alma 5:6–62)

Disney Animal Kingdom Florida

Epilogue

After living in Florida for six months, I am preparing to move to Utah, the land of Zion, to be closer to people of my own faith. I was able to become completely clean and sober for the longest time in my life, become worthy to receive the Melchizedek Priesthood and be ordained an elder in our church, enter the temple on Easter weekend and receive my temple endowment, and probably the greatest highlight was getting the opportunity to baptize Kimberly on Sunday, May 25, 2017. I thought that she had stopped going to church, but when she learned I would be leaving, as well as one of the sister missionaries who taught her completing her mission and returning home, she finally committed to becoming a member of Christ's church. I am so grateful we were able to experience this journey together. It was an honor to baptize her and one of the greatest feelings I have ever gotten to experience. She sent me this message as I am leaving, "I will be praying for you Ben, that you will have a safe and productive experience out there. I will really miss you. Sometimes, you don't really know how much you're going to miss someone until it's time for them to go. We will always be connected in this way."